One Day I'll Know

Joshua Crocker

ONE DAY I'LL KNOW

979-8-9879131-0-9 (paperback)

Library of Congress Control Number: 2023904894

Cover design by Joshua Crocker.

Classic version, paperback print. First edition 2023.

Published by the Paragon Coalition.
Norman, OK
paragoncoalition.com

Dedicated to…

The friends and family who inspired each word in this book. The relationships with you will always inspire my writing.

Preface *by Joshua Crocker*

I've always wanted to write. Some days it feels like I'm living in a world of my own, so I keep a pen nearby all the time so I can write down what it's like in my world.

When I first started writing, my hope was one day I would write my own novel. I was a storyteller, I used fiction to connect with the world. I was never a fan of poetry. To me poetry was just writing with rules. Despite that I took a crack at it when I wrote *The Pen, It's a Gateway*, what became my first poem. Because of my disdain for rules it was a free verse poem, of course. I wasn't completely swayed yet, but I grew a new appreciation for poetry over the months I wrote it.

It was July 2021 when I decided to pick up writing poetry again. I had written a couple of poems for various projects, but that had been about it. In a few weeks I would be turning seventeen and I had a lot on my mind at the moment. I told myself if I was going to try writing poetry I would do it my way. Each poem I would write like a song, imagining what it would be like to listen to the words as I drove home, windows down and the sun setting behind me.

You'll find my work inspired greatly by the music I listen to, from punk-rock to acoustic pop and a lot in between. I knew I wanted each song to be a few pages long, this way I could make a digital version of each song with a unique aesthetic I created using my graphic design skills.

So I started writing. Or more accurately started thinking about what I would write. I took a blue notebook with me on a camp that summer and came up with the idea for the first four songs I would write. From there, I spent the next year working on the poems in this book.

There's no doubt in my mind that writing the poems and songs in *One Day I'll Know* helped me grow and understand what it meant to be me. Nearly every word was written from July 2021 to July 2022, while I was seventeen. The songs explore many of the questions and thoughts I had as I was finding out who I was going to be. My faith, relationships, and just internal exploration influenced so much of my writing.

From my world to my pen, and for every question I have... one day I'll know.

One Day I'll Know

Act I

The part where I had it all figured out. Maybe.

The Pen, It's a Gateway By Joshua Crocker

In my hand I hold a key,
in my head I have a story,
in my heart is a dream,
and my eyes see the future gleam.

The ink splashes on the page
because my art, it's a getaway.
My thoughts become words
because the pen, it's a gateway.

Visions turn to reality,
the words inflict emotion.
Read between the lines,
see the characters shine,
it's supernatural and divine.

The mind is like an easel
creating the images of a story.
The canvas is the paper
making the movie reeling in your imagination.

An idea,
it's all you need
to be freed.

The ink splashes on the page
because my art, it's a getaway.
My thoughts become words
because the pen, it's a gateway.

Vivid imagery gives power to the senses.
Creativity can explode and break all fences.
They say an image is worth a thousand words,
I say a word is worth a million pictures.

A paper with a poem is full of life
and is an endless esse of emotion.
The heart is kind and love,
the dove is peace from above.
Fires of sin and the angered wrath,
the searching on his never-ending path.

Once you have the inspiration
your heart makes the creation.
Whatever inspires you,
it will be the bridge.
The wonders of your mind
are the world you live in.

In my hand I hold a key,
in my head I have a story,
in my heart is a dream,
and my eyes see the future gleam,
because the pen, it's a gateway.

Hey, Baby Brother By Joshua Crocker

Hey baby brother, I just gotta ask,
what's going on in your mind?
I mean, my head's like a rollercoaster,
a maze with no door to find.
But you stare up at me, just a calm look in your eyes.
I make faces down at you and see your smile light up.
Now I wonder what makes you tick,
all I do is worry about the next day,
y'know, whether God made each and every tree,
can I finish the year with all A's,
or if this girl would ever actually like me.
But you sit there now, just a calm look in your eyes.
Now I wonder what makes you tick,
I think maybe you're just happy being alive.

On the Fourth of July
the explosions shouted around us.
We all jumped in our excitement,
yet you didn't even bat your sleepy little eyes.
Fireworks lit the sky,
dreams soared as you lied.

Hey baby brother, I just gotta ask,
what's going on in your mind?
I mean, my head's like a rollercoaster,
a maze with no door to find.

Do you know how weird life will be?
You were born a month after an election,
our country tensed up at the reaction.
Your mom's smiling behind a mask,
horror or war, get ready to laugh,
each day will be the best till the last.

I'm a hotshot sixteen-year-old
trying to be the center of my world.
You're just a baby staring blankly
living in the center of your world.
But you stare up at me, just a calm look in your eyes.
I make faces down at you and see your smile light up.

Oh-oh-oh!
Hey baby brother, I just gotta ask.
Oh-oh-oh!
Hey baby brother, I just gotta ask.

Now I wonder what makes you tick.
Your little brain trying to make sense of it all,
each new place, each new way,
we're all telling you about it, you're experiencing it.
Do you understand any of the words I'm singin'?
Don't worry bro,
I hardly understand most of what I'm sayin'.

Now don't cry, things can get better,
that's what we're all wondering.
You've got it easy kid,
all I do is worry about the next day,
y'know, whether God made each and every tree,
can I finish the year with all A's,
or if this girl would ever actually like me.
That content look you give me,
it's quite admirable.
Next time I'll try to live in the now,
leave that doubt for tomor-row.

Hey baby brother, I just gotta ask,
what's going on in your mind?
I mean, my head's like a rollercoaster,
a maze with no door to find.
But you sit there now, just a calm look in your eyes.
Now I wonder what makes you tick.

Oh-oh-oh!
Hey baby brother, I just gotta ask.
Oh-oh-oh!
Hey baby brother, I just gotta ask.
Oh-oh-oh!
One day you'll know.

Hey baby brother, I just gotta ask,
what's going on in your mind?
I mean, my head's like a rollercoaster,
a maze with no door to find.
But you stare up at me, just a calm look in your eyes.
I make faces down at you and see your smile light up.
Now I wonder what makes you tick,
all I do is worry about the next day,
y'know, whether God made each and every tree,
can I finish the year with all A's,
or if this girl would ever actually like me.
But you sit there now, just a calm look in your eyes.
Now I wonder what makes you tick,
I think maybe you're just happy being alive.

Hey baby brother, I look down at you now,
I think maybe you're just happy being alive.
And y'know, so am I.

Act Like It By Joshua Crocker

Oooooh! You better listen up.
You preach love, but all I hear is blah-blah-blah.
You flash your smile and jaw-jaw-jaw. Ha!

It's as simple as 1, 2, forget the 3,
love thy neighbor as yourself.
But you don't act like it,
oh-no, you just don't act like it. Act like it.
You just don't act like it. Act like it.
Oh! Act like it. Act like it.

Trust me when I say your pretty smart,
damn, I wish I knew half of what you know.
Stories and tales, you seem to really care,
yet I feel you miss the point all the same.
C'mon we all know life is pretty hard,
trying to figure out who you want to be,
it'd be nice to know you're on my side.
What part of that is so fucking hard to understand?!

It's as simple as 1, 2, forget the 3,
love thy neighbor as yourself.
But you don't act like it,
oh-no, you just don't act like it. Act like it.
You just don't act like it. Act like it.
Oh! Act like it. Act like it.

Hey, I guess you give to the poor
and your faith quite literally moves mounts.
You've done really well at following Rule 1
but it's Rule 2 where you start to get hung,
it's then where you sound like a cymbal clangin'.
You think you're doing what's right and oh so simple
but we still hear the hate between the things you say,
the looks and the faults that we claim.

It's as simple as 1, 2, forget the 3,
love thy neighbor as yourself.
But you don't act like it,
oh-no, you just don't act like it. Act like it.
You just don't act like it. Act like it.
Oh! Act like it. Act like it.

C'mon, just shut up. (Shut up!)
You think you're living your pretty little life just right,
I'm here to tell you maybe not quite.

On Sunday you shine like the sun,
on Monday you smell like grime on the run.

You probably care more that I swore earlier in this song
than the fact you shun your own daughters and sons.
(Hell yeah, amiright!?)

It's as simple as 1, 2, forget the 3,
love thy neighbor as yourself.
But you don't act like it,
oh-no, you just don't act like it. Act like it.
You just don't act like it. Act like it.
Oh! Act like it. Act like it.

And I want to be honest,
I've been a bit confrontational
because the way you act makes me sad.
But I've got to act like it and show love,
so that's why I raise my hand to speak up,
I'll raise my voice until you hear what's up.
I know I'll make a difference with what I say,
the servant and leader about which I pray.

Here we go! Once more from the book,
you've heard it here before,
it's as simple as 1, 2, forget the 3,
love thy neighbor as yourself.
But you don't act like it,
why don't you act like it? Act like it.
You just don't act like it. Act like it.
Oh! Act like it. Act like it.
I'll love you till the day I die,
let's act like it.

I Can Write, But I Can't Sing By Joshua Crocker

La-la-la, la-la-la, la-la-laaaa,
la-la-la, la-la-la, la-la-la.
I can write the songs, but I cannot sing.
In my mind I'm the hero who saves everything.
But in reality, you know, well um, not so much.
La-la-la, la-la-la, la-la-laaaa.

I just had this great thought
redefining all that I've got,
but I don't quite understand the wording,
it's quite worrying,
taking what you know and what you say
and try to start sorting.
La-la-la!

Ring, ring, ring!
I can write, but I can't sing.
La-la-la-la-la-la-la!
No one wants to hear what was just sung,
the words get caught on my tongue,
roll off like a klutzy toddler on a diving board.
I just want to say what's on my mind
but I'm better with the pencil than the guitar.
So, if this song sounds bizarre
just remember, I can write, but I can't sing.
La-la-la, la-la-la, la-la-laaaa.

I'm singing in the shower,
the star of my Broadway musical.
Every conversation goes the perfect way,
the way they'd never go if I sung what to say.
Hey!

I'll sing it out in my car
when everyone is so far.
Do you ever feel like no one understands?
Nothing ever lands
because you can't find the perfect rhyme?
Then join the band.
La-la-la!

Ring, ring, ring!
I can write, but I can't sing.
La-la-la-la-la-la-la!
No one wants to hear what was just sung,
the words get caught on my tongue,
roll off like a drunk grandma on her back patio.
I just want to say what's on my mind
but I'm better with the pencil than the guitar.
So, if this song sounds bizarre
just remember, I can write, but I can't sing.
La-la-la, la-la-la, la-la-laaaa.

Ohhhhhhh!
Maybe if I hold the note, I won't screw it up.
Laaaaaaaaaaaaaaaa!
Guitar riff!
Ba-da-ba-ba-bo-err-yeah-la-oh-ba-ba-ah!
Woah!

I have the perfect thing to say,
I'll walk straight up and tell you,
but erp, there's a frog in my throat
and an excuse in my shoulder tote.
So, I won't sing, I'll keep writing,
live to fight another fighting,
I mean, fight to live on keeping,
or keep fighting to fight on living,
you get the point!

Oh, and: la-la-la!
Ring, ring, ring!
I can write, but I can't sing.
La-la-la-la-la-la-la!
No one wants to hear what was just sung,
the words get caught on my tongue,
roll off like a bronze-medalist on the pummel horse.
I just want to say what's on my mind
but I'm better with the pencil than the guitar.
So, if this song sounds bizarre
just remember, I can write, but I can't sing.
La-la-la, la-la-la, la-la-la,
la-la-la, la-la-la, la-la-la,
la-la-la, la-la-la, la-la-laaaa.

Here's the final verse,
hold your breath, it may be worse.
I can write the songs, but I cannot sing.
In my mind I'm the hero who saves everything.
But in reality, you know, well um not so much.
But the truth is, I love to sing,
I feel free and feel like me,
so bear with me as I complete the metaphor,
I know what I want to tell you and you
I just don't always have the words to say,
and when I'm in my room writing the words
everything sounds so great.
So, bear with me as I sing this song,
because it may not sound perfect,
but together we can love the beat.
La. La-la.
La-la-la, la-la-la, la-la-la.

The Song You'll Never Hear By Joshua Crocker

Is it a story that would ever be told?
I would wait by the front door for you
anxious as ever, twiddling my thumbs.
I had an eye when it came to silver or gold.
I started thinking of what to say
like fitting Tetris pieces in rhymes.

Every time you walked up, I'd say "hi,"
but to be fair I just like greeting everyone.
Anytime I make a joke I look to see what you say
because every smile gave me confidence to be me.

It's the song you'll never hear.
If only I had the courage,
the courage to tell you how I feel.
All the things I would sing during the chorus:
I'd let you know how pretty I find you,
how every damn thing you say makes me smile,
when you're around every problem goes away.

That week I was gone during the summer,
I started writing this song.
I thought of every lyric till it would make a melody.
I still had this unsettling doubt
that maybe I was just wrong.
I couldn't predict what'd you say,
but no matter what happens Saturday,
I just want you to know the truth.

You would hang by my side,
we laughed at the same things,
and before I ever could say a word,
you told me you weren't that person,
so I shut up and smiled along the rest of the night.
But when it was just you and me,
I looked into your eyes, and I was too nervous.
When you left, you waved bye,
and I couldn't stay sad.

I still like green,
does that make me funny and smart?
I'm here thinking about you
and drawing this heart.

It's the song you'll never hear.
If only I had the courage,
the courage to tell you how I feel.
All the things I would sing during the chorus:
I'd let you know how pretty I find you,
how every damn thing you say makes me smile,
when you're around every problem goes away.

There may be nothing special about you,
but to me you're the cutest girl around.
Given the chance I would flirt with you all day.
Every few seconds I glance your way,
I get nervous in the best way around you.

I still have your phone number saved
from the one week where the future looked paved.
I didn't expect to say a thing,
because I never expected to see you then,
but in the end, I took a chance
and you came along for the ride.
It didn't last long,
but for a second you were by my side.
Damnit.

How many chances did I blow?
I could never get the nerve to say anything to you.
Now I walk to my car cussing, "fucking shit."
I sit in the dark, this time all alone.

At this point I don't even know
if I'm afraid of failure
or just scared of the risk.
What a sad way to live your life.

It's the song you'll never hear.
If only I had the courage,
the courage to tell you how I feel.
All the things I would sing during the chorus:
I'd let you know how pretty I find you,
how every damn thing you say makes me smile,
when you're around every problem goes away.

Did you ever realize the way I felt?
Would it have even made a difference?
I hate the way I miss seeing you,
you could always light up my day.

I can make excuses like a story with no ending
but I can't sing a song with the beat missing.
If I saw you again, would I finally listen,
or would I let you wave goodbye again?

It's the song you'll never hear.
If only I had the courage,
the courage to tell you how I feel.
All the things I would sing during the chorus:
I'd let you know how pretty I find you,
how every damn thing you say makes me smile,
when you're around every problem goes away.
Every problem except one:
and it's this stupid song I'm writing.

...

Shit, people say I lie too much,
but honestly, I'm just afraid of the truth.

Damn Wind By Joshua Crocker

Damn wind hitting my face,
blowing my thoughts across the park.
Opportunity doesn't come in a steady stream,
it rushes in like a roaring wave.
Never felt more alive,
the air in my hair,
a paper capering pen,
the current of life sweepin' in.
Damn wind keeps pushing me thin,
it blows open the door
and I have to pull it shut.
Oh, shit. *Ha-ha*

Shuffle the deck for me,
then deal them out face down,
because I keep my cards close to my chest.
I'll plan my next move here tonight,
strategize what's right.
Don't let the wind take that away.

Damn rain soaking my coat,
dripping my hopes across the bus.
Tomorrow's chances won't wait for another day,
they pour on you till your shivering cold.
Never felt more alive,
the air in my hair,
a paper capering pen,
the current of life sweepin' in.
Damn wind keeps pushing me thin,
it blows open the door
and I have to pull it shut.
Oh, shit. *Ha-ha*

I don't mind blaming it on the rain
and I won't stop cussing at the wind.
I can't wait for Friday,
so I can wish that it were Monday again.

Damn sun blinding my eyes,
taking my words across the world.
A week to find words you can't say when your nervous,
say it when the sun sets or watch the stars at home.
Never felt more alive,
the air in my hair,
a paper capering pen,
the current of life sweepin' in.
Damn wind keeps pushing me thin,
it blows open the door
and I have to pull it shut.
Oh, shit. *Ha-ha*

I'll save the best for last,
and wait for the perfect moment,
like a slight breeze in a sunset-lit sky,
but this ain't my perfect world,
and if you wait until the end,
chances are it'll never come.

That damn wind.
Blowing highway speed 95,
I don't got the time
for monsoons, cyclones, and gales too.

Opportunity comes a rollin',
I hear a knock at the door,
I'm afraid to go outside,
because the wind might take it away.
I don't want to win if I might lose.
It's the game I'm playing,
the irony is you see...
I always lose anyway.

Damn wind hitting my face,
blowing my thoughts across the park.
Opportunity doesn't come in a steady stream,
it rushes in like a roaring wave.
Never felt more alive,
the air in my hair,
a paper capering pen,
the current of life sweepin' in.
Damn wind keeps pushing me thin,
it blows open the door
that I have to pull shut.
Oh... shit.
And that ain't the wind, it's me.

Damn.

i'm still afraid of the dark By Joshua Crocker

during the day i complain about the sun,
its heat beating against my skin.
during the day i'm busy; never quite done.

when night falls i'm left alone,
my thoughts echo through my brain,
stuck in a maze; my time to atone.

i'm still afraid of the dark,
monster eyes peaking from my closet,
quick, turn on the lamp.
i hear a rattle down the hall,
a shake under the bed,
emptiness surrounds me.

when the day's done stars shine at last,
just me and my thoughts are left.
there's nothing that terrifies me like that.

is tonight another ticket on the train ride?
a stop by all my normal places:
regret, doubt, and discontent. do i hide?

some nights i decide to be a hero in skies higher,
some evenings i'm a disastrous lovesick villain,
it's a story of where i hope with a voice of desire.

a monster hides itself closest to me,
my mind is trapped there in the closet,
it reminds me of everything absentee.

i'm still afraid of the dark,
monster eyes peaking from my closet,
quick, turn on the lamp.
i hear a rattle down the hall,
a shake under the bed,
emptiness surrounds me.

where the light goes it will mislead,
i use my hope like a drug,
a strange sense of optimism indeed.

a bruised rib is nothing to a broken heart to be reckoned.
i rather get punched in the face ten times
than be left alone with my thoughts for a second.

memories are the mind's greatest lie,
moments that no longer exist
left there just to remind you to cry.

lay awake at night, try to be the first to sleep,
or if i have the imagination to distract myself,
maybe i won't let all the broken parts of me seep.

i'm still afraid of the dark,
monster eyes peaking from my closet,
quick, turn on the lamp.
i hear a rattle down the hall,
a shake under the bed,
emptiness surrounds me.

you know why every night i sleep with the lights on?
i happily spend a lot of time by myself,
but being alone scares the shit out of me till dawn.

i don't know if i want to sleep tonight,
because in the morning i won't want to get up,
not until i see the kitchen lights get bright.

during the day i tour a park,
the music of the sun takes me away,
why am i'm still afraid of the dark?

dear lord, will you love me every day?
i flip flop on how great i say i am,
will you make me better i pray.

i'm still afraid of the dark,
monster eyes peaking from my closet,
quick, turn on the lamp.
i hear a rattle down the hall,
a shake under the bed,
emptiness surrounds me.

a star is a light in the darkest of evening skies.

My Worst Nemesis By Joshua Crocker

The clock strikes twelve.
My dear we face off again.
Back and forth, we'll trade blows.
You've put me through Heaven and Hell.
You're like a nasty kick to the shin,
but that's just how this story goes.
...
You may already know him.
It's my old friend,
the consequences of my own actions.

Oh, how I hate him so.
The little fucker follows me wherever I go.
If I try to eat an ice cream pint
my stomach churns like a hurricane.
Oh, the pain!
You leave your clothes in a pile of lint
and they wrinkle overnight. What?!

I began tying my shoe while driving
and my car went to the curb careening.
I was talking with a pal and started lying,
and now everything they say is demeaning.
People, c'mon?!

I won't rest until justice is wrought,
and I can get away with shit without
dealing with what all these consequences brought.

Skipped a project for a day (month) or so
and now I have to do it all in an hour or fail?
How does any of this (that) seem fair?
Why should I be responsible? Is it too late to bail?

Concentrate, passively.
Procrastinate, catastrophe.

Last time I slept in till nine,
I wasted two hours of the day.
If only the sun knew my plan.
Also, where did all the hot water go?
I was only in the shower for half an hour, ya know.

Jumped off the couch,
broke my ankle.
Jumped on the couch,
broke the couch.
Make up your mind.

Oh, the consequences of my own actions,
you keep me on the edge of my seat.
You don't like me,
and buddy I definitely don't like you.

Like they say, I was a liar, liar,
now my fucking pants are on fire.
Does anyone have an extinguisher?
Or at least a bucket of water?
I guess this will be the last time I play with matches.
Maybe my pants just need fireproof patches?
Now there's a good idea...

I was playing with a ball inside
and that's when I broke mom's lamp,
Good thing they invented tape, amiright?
I'm so clever, I know.
On that note, I went for a run in the snow,
turns out now I have a cold,
my nose just keeps dripping gold.
Snot. By gold I meant snot.
Just clarifying.

Newton said for every action
there is an equal and opposite reaction.
In response I have come to the conclusion:
screw that.

Why is it my choices are my responsibility?
My, you are so keen on hostility.
Do I own what I do the same,
when I have a finger for pointing blame?
Maybe I'm at fault,
ugh, it tastes like salt.

I so hate consequences,
you're my worst nemesis,
a monster of my own creation.
Damn, I guess I got to fix this.

The Song You'll Never Hear (Reprise) By J. Crocker

It had been so long, so I texted you just to say hi.
After waiting a half hour you texted back.
Damn, why was I always so eager to wait.
I asked what's new with you
and you told me about your new boy.

It's the song you'll never hear.
I never had the courage,
the courage to tell you how I feel.
I sing to myself now a chorus:
You'll never know how pretty I find you,
the time every damn thing you said made me smile,
when you were around every problem went away.
You're not around anymore are you.

I said it was neat, that was a lie.
Reality is I just sat there and cried.
I don't think you'll ever know
how much I hung on every word you said.

"Indeed."
Fuck off I thought.
A word stuck like a dagger.

It's the song you'll never hear.

With my heart broken,
the days when I could count on your laugh are gone.
I'll finish this song tears in my eyes.
Now these inches feel like a mile.
I'm sorry. *i'm sorry*
I shouldn't have let someone like you go.
It hurts now, but thinking of you
will always make me smile.

...

Shit, people say I lie too much.
Maybe it's for the best.

My Last Christmas By Joshua Crocker

It's only October and my family is already asking me what I want for Christmas. I meant to write things down as the year went by, but July came and went and now here we are. I wish I could give you all my wishes, but I have more important shit now. I've never been a gift person anyway.

I'm not ready for Christmas to pass, because what if it's my last? If I grow up, will all the magic be lost? All I want for Christmas is to sit around the tree. Let the fireplace thaw all the memories for me.

I'm seventeen now. Graduation and New Years are in sight. That first Christmas you held me; did you imagine how I would turn out? Are you proud of the young man I'm becoming? You raised and cared for me; you woke up early to hide those last presents under the tree. Are you ready for me to start my own life, or are you as terrified as me?

There's something special about Thanksgiving, whether I'm watching the Macy's Day Parade, or the Lions lose. I spent the week imagining what my next step would be. Downtown and turkey, family and working. If I'm about to turn the page on my life, what will I name the next chapter?

This time of year will always be my favorite. But I only have five weeks of school left, so... And I keep finding myself at work more and more often. To be fair, I love what I do. Shit, I definitely will help hang ornaments with you this evening, but I might need to make a few stops on my way home. I'd love to watch *It's Christmas Charlie Brown* on Saturday, but my weekends are filled till the Eve. I can't wait to guess what's in the presents under the tree, but I have my own shopping list now. The advent may last for twenty-five days, but I only have twenty-four hours in a day. This time of year will always be my favorite, but I let time pass so fast.

In the past my friends and I would head down to see the lights, sparklin' and shinin'. We would walk around laughin' and talkin'. I fell and ripped my pants and now I still tell the story. We were kids and for some reason I thought those times would never end. I was too busy growing up to see you all doing the same. Do you feel as lost as me without each other? He moved out and moved on. She can't escape her own demons. Fuck if I know what I'm doing without any of you. I haven't talked to him in years. I wish she and I were closer, but now work and school keep her busy. Now I walk the streets looking at the lights without you guys. Maybe I've got someone new, but the times with you are what I fondly knew. Hey, I guess we all grew up at least.

I'm not ready for Christmas to pass, because what if it's my last? If I grow up, will all the magic be lost? All I want for Christmas is to sit around the tree. Let the fireplace thaw all the memories for me.

Every year the taste of peppermint and chocolate rushes in the holiday spirit. But right now, all I can do is think about a girl that I let go to soon because the truth made me fear it. I can't stop wishing your head was on my shoulder. As the cold December breeze fills the air, I would give my jacket to hold her. Anymore it's dark out and I sit alone in my car drinking my shake, looking to the right. I still remember when you were sitting next to me in the passenger seat, but now memories are all I have of that night.

Caroling in the living room at Grammy's house, every year we get excited for it. There's nothing like a sleigh ride with you. The kids host the show and it's the performance of the year. Every season it seems to be harder and harder to get prepared, I reckon. Imagine a string, pulling each and all of us in different directions. Will life steal what the holiday beckons?

What will I miss most once the fireworks die and it's January? I miss the wonder I had when I was younger. How many missed decisions have I made off of hypotheticals? Did I miss the right path because I was looking for a laugh? I've missed many shots, more than I'll ever know. Miss, I'm starting to realize I think more than I show. That's enough! If I keeping fretting about what I'll miss then I'd lose time to smile, and I rather smile at every snowflake falling then the ones melting. But damnit. I miss you.

When I leave home, everyone likes me but who is there to love me? If I'm well-liked and a leader, I'm afraid it's lonely at the top. When all my friends are freshman will I have to start over? Shit, now I feel ungrateful, because even if I've got life like the presents waiting for me, I'm still grasping at what I lost. If this is who I want to be, why is it okay that I don't know if it's the me that had all those dreams?

I'm not ready for Christmas to pass, because what if it's my last? If I grow up, will all the magic be lost? All I want for Christmas is to sit around the tree. Let the fireplace thaw all the memories for me.

When all is said and done, there's only so many days left in the year. It's up to me now to make time for what I love. I'll enjoy the holiday and not worry about next year, ha, not yet anyway. Tears, wonders, fears, ponders. Heartbreak hurts so much, but it's not the wins that make me who I am, but the losses. When it's time to make resolutions, I can smile knowing this year I came out battered and bruised, but still on top.

Hey mom and dad, thanks. All the presents were nice, but it isn't the unwrapping that I'll remember, but the people smiling this morning in December. You prepared me for the best and I'll be back for the worst. I'm still worried, but you tell me I'll always make you proud and I don't plan on changing that.

I may be not ready for Christmas to pass, but it's here now. I'm about to grow up, where will the magic go? Smile now, because we're all sitting around the tree. The fireplace will thaw all the memories for me.

One Day I'll Know

Act II

The part where I wasn't quite as sure.

One Day I'll Know By Joshua Crocker

I think a lot of thoughts,
my questions are suggestions.
I'm a smart kid, 32 on the ACT, GPA above 4.0,
but now that I've grown up a bit,
I'm not sure I know a thing,
I haven't got this life thing figured out,
but it has got me wondering...

Ohhhh-la-di-loh-ho. Oh!

My parents love me so much they gave me two homes.
Relationships are where the complications hit.
Do best friends really last forever?
Because I hardly know who mine are anymore.
You see, there's another girl I am friends with
and I wonder if she has the same feelings for me.
How do you draw a line
between loneliness and friendliness?
Am I my best friend? I hope not, I'm annoying as heck.
I'm sure one day I'll know.

Ohhhh...
One day I'll know what life's got in store,
and one day I'll know what's behind that old door,
oh, one day I'll know where my feet are leading me,
they keep leading me,
to places I want to see,
my thoughts keep telling me,
things I don't quite believe,
and one day I'll know what it means.

Ohhhh-la-di-loh-ho. Oh!

This, that, be the change you want to see in the world.
Transformation is just new ways of frustration.
Is change ever actually real?
Because there is still hate, poverty, and war.
You see, the people in charge just don't care
and I wonder if I even care enough to fight it.
How do you make a difference
when enough of this is real tough?
Is there any hope? I'm going to keep trying anyway.
I'm sure one day I'll know.

Ohhhh...
One day I'll know what life's got in store,
and one day I'll know what's behind that old door,
oh, one day I'll know where my feet are leading me,
they keep leading me,
to places I want to see,
my thoughts keep telling me,
things I don't quite believe,
and one day I'll know what it means.

Ohhhh-la-di-loh-ho. Oh!

The more my faith grows, it feels like the less I know.
Love unaltered is hardly ever unfaltered.
Am I the one who believes what's wrong?
Because few people share what I see, here and there.
You see, love's been replaced with fear and control
and I wonder if that's truth or if there's answer in prayer.
How do you trust more
in the doubt than dying in the lying?
Who do I love most? Me, you, Jesus, or all the above.
I'm sure one day I'll know.

Ohhhh...
One day I'll know what life's got in store,
and one day I'll know what's behind that old door,
oh, one day I'll know where my feet are leading me,
they keep leading me,
to places I want to see,
my thoughts keep telling me,
things I don't quite believe,
and one day I'll know what it means.

Ohhhh-la-di-loh-ho. Oh!

As a kid I loved mazes, cool thing is that's life!
Situations, you wonder about expectations.
Will today be the best day ever?
Because I'm feeling unsure of where I'm going.
You see, ambitious hopes leave you exhausted
and I wonder if I have what it takes to be me.
Am I the best teacher,
writer, or person for to be certain?
Hey, are you ready? That's the question I keep asking me.
I'm sure one day I'll know.

I suppose it will all make sense when we grow up.

Ohhhh...
One day I'll know what life's got in store,
and one day I'll know what's behind that old door,
oh, one day I'll know where my feet are leading me,
they keep leading me,
to places I want to see,
my thoughts keep telling me,
things I don't quite believe,
and one day I'll know what it means.

I've got all these questions in my head,
there's all these thoughts in the air here.
Ohhhh-la-di-loh-ho.
Uncertainty can certainly be scary,
but I know I'll figure out how this next part goes.
Ohhhh-la-di-loh-ho.
Ohhhh... one day I'll know!
Ohhhh-la-di-loh-ho.

One day I'll know.
Oh, one day I'll know.
One day I'll know.
Oh, one day I'll know.
One day I'll know.
Sigh, one day I'll know.

The Trouble Is By Joshua Crocker

There's a trouble everyone's been hearing about
and yet not a single soul is talking this.
It's easier to stay quiet than speak up,
and that right there is what the trouble is.

Y'know this is all real troublin',
everything seems to be bubblin',
when all's gone to shit, we won't stand tall,
this trouble's here and all of us just stall,
we won't say things or do the what be done,
and that right there is what the trouble is.

Stand around as we say damn you all to hell,
but we won't say a word about the hell we've made fall.
There's something wrong and we ain't done a thing,
sayin' nothing right now will cause more harm to us all.

Y'all are so preachy that everything is so peachy.
What if we stopped to talk it all out,
maybe instead of crying themselves to sleep,
we could figure out an end to all the doubt.

Y'know this is all real troublin',
everything seems to be bubblin',
when all's gone to shit, we won't stand tall,
this trouble's here and all of us just stall,
we won't say things or do the what be done,
and that right there is what the trouble is.

It's the topics we avoid like a plague.
Hey, we all need to toughen up buttercup,
you can say it makes you feel icky,
but when trouble comes here, it's time to speak up.

I feel sad for you if your thoughts are on lock,
you say being vulnerable is pretty bad.
Investigating things, like what's going on all around,
is how you get to being the person who's glad.

Y'know this is all real troublin',
everything seems to be bubblin',
when all's gone to shit, we won't stand tall,
this trouble's here and all of us just stall,
we won't say things or do the what be done,
and that right there is what the trouble is.

Topical nonsense is a frightening defense,
excuses for nothing is what you come up
with when you plan it,
but for everything leave it unchanged,
you so don't want to hear it you rather say ban it.

Sit down with those who listen to you,
and hear them, hear all that they have to say.
Let's talk about it. Let's get over this trouble.
This storm's still a brewin', so don't fray.

Y'know this is all real troublin',
everything seems to be bubblin',
when all's gone to shit, we won't stand tall,
This trouble's here and all of us just stall,
we won't say things or do the what be done,
and that right there is what the trouble is.
That's what the trouble is.

Shopping Mall By Joshua Crocker

Welcome all to a haven of the new,
replace all you knew with a shiny toy!
Gather around ladies and gents, cause boy,
it's a place where all your wildest dreams come true!

Years go by now,
all the signs fall from the limelight,
I'm losing my grasp of reality.
When it's just you and me.

Save me, I'm dying.
Save me, I'm dying.
Save me, I'm dying.
Save me, I'm dying.
Save me, I'm dying.

Welcome all to a hell unknown to you,
everything once new is a rotting ploy!
Gather around ladies and gents, cause boy,
it's a place where all your finalist dreams come true!

We'll make out under the flickering lights.
When it's just you and me.

Save me, I'm dying.
Save me, I'm dying.
Save me, I'm dying.
Save me, I'm dying.
Save me, I'm dying.

I'll take your heart in a trickling fight.
Now it's just you and me.

Save me, I'm dying.
Save me, I'm dying.
Save me, I'm dying.
Save me, I'm dying.
Save me, I'm dying.

Just one night will be enough,
just one day will leave you here,
my joyous cry echoes down the halls,
your lasting happiness shall be what falls.

Smell the scent of yesterday,
I'll eat it straight up.
Smell the fear we have,
I'll eat you straight up.
We always find new ways.
We'll eat. We'll eat. We'll eat!
You'll go down to the shops together,
save me a seat.

Hip-hip-hooray! Go away!
Come back another day!
We have sales that will make you pay,
we'll sell your mind into our fray.
Hehehehehehe!

Lovely day we're having!
Savings will have you dying.
Join the carousel of time
semi-adjacent to the food court of hell.
Three stories, escalators, fire facades,
elevators, stairs, shelters, and you.
Now now,
no more fashioning dashing escapes.

Will someone save me?
Just not them.
Just not them.
Just not them.
I'm talking about you!

Hip-hip-hooray! Go away!
Don't come back another day!
We hate you in the same.
You hate you all the same.
I hate and love you the same.

Hi, welcome you cutie.
Hi, welcome to beauty.
Hi, welcome to fresher deals.
Hi, welcome to flashy meals.
Hi, welcome to your wonder.
Hi, welcome to our plunder.
Hi, welcome to insanity.
Hi, welcome to calamity.
Hi, welcome to the end.
Hi, welcome my friend.

GO AWAY!
I'm dying.
No I'm not.

Save me, we're dying.
Save me, we're dying.
Save me, we're dying.
Save me, we're dying.
Save me, we're dying.

Graffiti runs down my teary face,
what have you done to me?
Who are we, you fool, would you know who?
Vandals of the night, sinners in our eyes,
you're you is what belongs to who.
Who is we, love is high, your end is nigh.
Captives in a hellscape, your mind trying to escape,
your body dwelling further in mistake.

Bye, hell comes at the end.
Bye, hell comes my friend.

Save me, I'm dying.
Save me, I'm dying.
Save me, I'm dying.
Save me, I'm dying.
Save me, we're dying.

Save me, please. Please save me.
I can't take it anymore.
Don't leave. When it's too late, I'm dying.

Welcome all to a haven of the new.
Welcome all to a hell unknown to you.
Save me, I'm dying.
Replace all you knew with a shiny toy.
Everything once new is a rotting ploy.
Save me, I'm dying.
Gather around ladies and gents, cause boy,
it's a place where all your finalist dreams come true!
Save me, you're dying.

Ahhhahhahahhhahahhhah!

Middle America By Joshua Crocker

Welcome to the land of the free,
where every week we shop for a
buy three, get one free.
This is a tribute to the great folks
of the suburban dream.
God bless Middle America!

They told me buy low, sell high,
my friends rather just get high.
They told me all about the good ol' days
but welcome to the present days, (hip-hooray!)
where instead you sell what you got
and buy dirt because you're a filthy dot.
Mud in the air, cracks in the streets.
If we squint past that,
we may just see your make-believe,
and now I see a land of dreams!
Yesterday's future is here! (see!)

We're the upper-lower-middle class types,
the Middle American heroes on the 9 to 5,
driving down the freeway goin' fifty-five.

We don't care what's
north-eyed, eastbound, southside, west wound.
We got our Taco Bells and 7-Elevens,
we ain't livin' easy, but we're no starvin' city.
We fill the stands at baseball games,
buy cheap beer before football games.

The suburban sprawl is our mark,
the cozy homes and everyday streets,
nothing ever happens after dark,
fast food if you want some eats.
I love it here! (no, seriously)

I drove past 27 churches on my way to the supermarket,
bought some milk, bread, and OJ,
it's been quite the day.
They're doing construction on the train tracks,
whole town's in gridlock here and back.

Those government fat cats keeping takin' my money,
we all agree that taxes get the axes honey!
Y'know, if we forget about
the kids in our schools hangin' by a thread,
and the pilin' medical bills, and college debt,
that are my darn constitutional right,
then maybe we can finally get some rest at night.

Like a patch in your jeans, we'll fix the infrastructure,
make Middle America shine across
this great country of ours!
I don't take the bus 'cuz I don't like people,
give me a car and some tunes to venture the sprawl.
Be your own boss, an entrepreneur of sorts,
all you need is an idea to tack on
(and a loan from ya local bank)
and you can make it great!

Middle America is a lie from up there above
and I ain't talking about the God you love,
they steal from you and leave you the poor.
Our suburban home is a mess you can't ignore,
contentment for crooks leave us all spiralin',
ain't it a stank of a bunch of malarkalin'.

My love lives in the suburbs,
my family dines in the Braum's diner down the street.
Order a pizza or see a movie on the weekend,
hide away in the semi-pretty parks
and the back of the li-berry.
It's the quiet life that I find worth the seek.

Welcome to the land of the free,
pollution is our solution,
inflation our incarceration,
but it's the perfect home for me.
This is a tribute to the great folks
of the suburban dream.
God bless Middle America!

Little White Lies By Joshua Crocker

"Don't listen to them Joshua,
I'm the one who really loves you."

Your little white lies,
you're the ghost inside my mirror.
Your little white lies,
I'm drowning in my fears.

I ask about your day, you say:
"Good, how about you?"
Really though? I can't believe you,
or even worse, what I say:
"I'm doin' alright."
What?! Is that real though?
You don't care to be honest,
but do I really care about you?
The whole world is run by little white lies,
and the one person I can turn to
is the ghost inside my mirror.

A smiling friend will hurt you more,
an enemy scoffs at your pain,
motivation comes from the last,
let your guard down only if you dare,
because the voice you hear comes from there.

Your little white lies,
you're the ghost inside my mirror.
Your little white lies,
the whisper in my ears.

Don't we all need some peace and quiet,
time to myself leaves me stronger,
I can keep running longer.
I can't trust people
and the way their gears turn,
or the day their fears churn.
It's the things I can't see.
What I can rationalize is code,
and if nothing else abodes to you,
I hear the ghost tell me who is who.

The silver tongue sings me a melody,
the beautifully eerie song of sirens.
Betrayal stabs in me in the back,
and when I'm alone, I'll know who.
Find it there, in the illusions of the mind.

Your little white lies,
you're the ghost inside my mirror.
Your little white lies,
the sorrow in my tears.

It's not the supernatural that runs high,
in life it's the natural I'll fight,
every day till it's right. There's my fight.
I can make this work before it gets worse.
I'm the best I've got,
or so I've been told.
Ghastly confusion and my true conclusion is this:
I look in the mirror to find my next step,
only to find myself behind where I was,
my very thought spun on like a top.

I'm looking for somewhere I belong,
yet I'm lost in a labyrinth of glass,
running around, searching for nothing.
You tell me I'm fine.
You can stop lying.
Ghosts haunt day and night,
call it what we may,
but if I don't know what's true,
do I really know you?

You get me drunk on my hope,
a fantasy I'll never hold.
But when my mind sobers up,
I call you for the bullshit you really are.

Your little white lies,
you're the ghost inside my mirror.
Your little white lies,
you're the friend who endears,
the enemy who sneers,
and your voice is always near.

Sunspot Freckles By Joshua Crocker

I gaze at your sunspot freckles,
you have the beauty of a spectacle,
your dress as lovely as a solar flare.
When you smile, I know you care,
and I wonder to myself,
can an aurora shine as bright as you?

When I'm with you I'm with the stars,
you glow as bright as the red reflection of Mars.
Your love travels lightspeed,
I wouldn't want to be anywhere but here.

I need to tell you space is cold,
I travel down the path of life in darkness.
As I fly closer to you,
your joyous rays fill me with warmth
and light wipes away the void.

I gaze at your sunspot freckles,
you have the beauty of a spectacle,
your dress as lovely as a solar flare.
No one else radiates like you.

All the wonders of the spectrum
reflect off your beautiful hair.
Your voice resounds a calming hum
and when you smile, I know you care.

I lie in my backyard across the grass,
I look towards the Heavens and watch the sky,
you stare out your window to look up.
Just remember, in the vastness seen above
is the same comet you and I both love.

Your heart sets the ice ablaze,
your laugh is the glistening star,
your lucent love fills my dreams.
The thought of you glints in my mind.

I gaze at your sunspot freckles,
the joyous gold glowing in your cheeks,
is that of the brightest light of the sun.

A spectrum is within all life.
What will you reflect? That is what shows.
A heart of fire will mirror love to all.

I gaze at your sunspot freckles,
you have the beauty of a spectacle,
your dress as lovely as a solar flare.

All the mysteries of space,
all the questions in the universe,
but I just wonder to myself,
can an aurora shine as bright as you?

Depths of Sin By Joshua Crocker

The forest is full of turns,
I walk unsure of where I am
and all I have to show is the burns.

The howls of the wolves chase me,
the thorns rise from the dirt to snare me.
I retreat to a cave only to find nothing,
nothing but this lost soul of mine,
a soul that has fallen in the depths of sin.

I sit forgotten and unloved by the world,
I fall to the ground, filled with doubt.
All hope has departed from me here,
yet I hear your call in the distance
and I know you are near.

"Please," I pray,
"Save me from this place,
bring me back to your love."

Your tender voice sooths my ears,
you tell me to come,
don't live in the dark anymore,
you will protect me now.

Your light guides me through the trees,
my heart wishes to be with you.
The wolves lunge at me,
yet you shield me under your wings.

With your words piercing the air,
I know I'll never be lost.
When night brings dark thoughts,
I know you'll protect and care.

When life knocks me over, I'll stand back up.
When life pushes me down, I'll stand back up.
When I have no legs left to walk on,
you will carry me upon your shoulder.

Through your sacrifice I am new,
and through your love I have hope.
One day I will finally make it,
make it to the golden gate.
On that day I'll live my life with you.

I sit forgotten and unloved by the world,
I fall to the ground, filled with doubt.
Yet when I pray for your love,
I know nothing will ever harm me.

Leave Me Alone By Joshua Crocker

Leave me alone. Leave me alone.
Will you please just leave me alone?!
Just shut up, won't you? Please.

Morning: I wake up.
Best part of the day for an optimist;
you got the whole day ahead of you.
I'm still not entirely awake,
so I'll enjoy my breakfast in peace
with a screen and no screams from you.

An hour-ish later: You get chatty.
Maybe I'm writing or in a class,
perhaps running an errand or just relaxing.
But you're so full of it, you and your sass.
Ha, we'll joke around, a zing from you.
You and your stupid smile. You're still an ass.

Do you really think I'm stupid?
Like I don't know who I am,
because you remind me of every little thing,
I think what you think is enough,
and I've had it with your high and mighty pride.
Guess what kid, you don't know shit, huh!

Leave me alone. Leave me alone.
Will you please just leave me alone?!
Just shut up, won't you? Please.

Time by yourself is nice, I'd say.
Introversion's curse is your recursion.
Girls, work, eating, faith, and news.
Sports, numbers, creativity, and you.
It's a bit much to take in, don't you think?
Because you always are. You always are. *Sigh*.

Afternoon: You're still there, aren't you?
I wouldn't know, I'd rather ignore you.
Evening: People are around.
It's nice to have someone else to talk to.

When this is all too much, I go where it's calm.
But you're still there. You're always here.
I can get away from everyone else
but you never go away. All I need is a break.

Leave me alone. Leave me alone.
Will you please just leave me the fuck alone?!
You always have something to say.
That's enough. Just shut up. Please.

Why are you my enemy anyway?
Can't we just be friends
because when we get along,
things don't feel so wrong.
Let's call it a peace treaty,
take a break from the overthinking
and get back to singing.

Enough of the fighting,
I'm alone with my thoughts.
…
"So, what's next?"

Do You Like Me? By Joshua Crocker

Do you like me?
Because right now I'm not sure you do.
Tell me all the great things,
which I don't believe.
Do you like me?
Cuz, I'm waiting for you to say so.

I'm a cocky superstar
rocking this place!
My inspiration takes me far,
the word hero comes to mind,
the main character in my life's story.
I know I'm great, at least I think I do,
that's what's true and you have no clue.

Oh! Welcome to my life,
my unearned confidence and I
taking center stage.
Oh! Grab the mic please,
let me ask, do you like me?

Say it to my face and I won't believe you,
I want to know what you say behind my back,
the reassurance of my greatness.
I mean, I know how great I am,
I just want to make sure you do too.

Are you proud of me?
I gave it my all, just to hear you say,
hey, you did amazing today.
I think I'm so smart and talented,
are you proud of me?
Cuz, I'm waiting for you to say so.

I see myself as a shining knight,
I mean, I've got the charisma,
I won't back down from a fight
with my words as sharp as a sword.
It's time to be my dream hero,
what to do isn't so clear though.
Slaying a dragon is surprisingly hard
when you can't read the map to his lair.
I may see myself as a shining knight,
but in the end, the knight gets the girl,
and I don't.

Oh! Welcome to my life,
my unearned confidence and I
taking center stage.
Oh! Grab the mic please,
let me ask, do you like me?

I'm not a greedy guy,
I just want the one thing I can't have,
and I blame myself for what I call a loss.
I expect the world of me
and when the world doesn't deliver,
am I the one to blame a loser?
A question of paradoxical theory,
can a winner like me lose
or is that who I am to you?

Do you love me?
Because of course you do, (I'm great)
and nothing I ever do is what changes that,
so why am I worried with impressing you?
Do you love me?
Cuz, I'm waiting for you to say so.

Why do people keep telling me what I want to hear?
Or maybe I say those things to avoid these fears.
Why do I think what I know I don't want to hear?
It's all very weird.

Oh! Welcome to my life,
my unearned confidence and I
taking center stage.
Oh! Grab the mic please,
let me ask, do you like me?

These questions may sound stupid
but deep down I know they're not for you.
Why do you think I need reassurance from you,
unless I wasn't so sure my words are true?
Do I like myself, is what I really want to know.
Unearned confidence is a mask
for thoughts I keep saying aren't a low.

Do you like me?
Because everything you say tells me you do.
You tell me these great things,
why don't I believe you?
Do you like me?
Because I'm not so sure if I do.

Therapist By Joshua Crocker

I don't trust therapists. What kind of human profits from other people's misery? They're the lawyers of the mind, the psychos of the psyche.

```
```

I'm not lost, but I don't have it all figured out. I wonder if I could use therapy. Probably could be a benefit to someone like me.

My life is going great, and I won't shut up about it. I lose count of everything I'm happy about. Haha, deep down I know I'm a spoiled brat. Ain't that the shit.

But in case you're new to this whole life thing, I'll let you know. Everyday wear comes for free. My sleep schedule is fine except when it isn't. I keep myself busy because otherwise I just feel tired. Sometimes nothing sounds good, and I don't always eat well. I'll still love you though.

My mind knows emotional variance and emotional awareness. Introspection comes with retrospection. I don't need help (at least not from you), so shut your mouth. I like the idea of therapy, but I hate therapists.

```
```

I don't trust therapists. What kind of human profits from other people's misery? They're the lawyers of the mind, the psychos of the psyche.

```
```

I'm not even eighteen and three of my friends have tried to kill themselves. I count myself lucky they've all failed so far.

I become desensitized to pain when it's all around me. I once held a girl only to look down and see the cuts and scars. I knew in the moment what she told me would be worsening. I wrote a letter to another; did you get it? My best friend spiraled out of control. Against all odds, I keep standing tall.

I'm tired of seeing texts asking me what I'd do if you tried to kill you. I'm tired of getting told to find you in a hospital. I'm tired of looking in my friends' eyes, hearing them talk, but finding nothing there. I'm just tired.

```
```

I don't trust therapists. What kind of human profits from other people's misery? They're the lawyers of the mind, the psychos of the psyche.

```
```

I prefer living life alone. Ha, and I wonder why I'm so lonely. I won't open up to you because I leave myself vulnerable. The words we say to each other are unalterable. I wasn't lying when I said my biggest fear was the truth.

Music is my therapy. Poems are my counseling. I'm honest with myself, otherwise I wouldn't be writing anymore, so why should I be honest with you?

Therapists and their cruel ears. A notebook to write down my flaws. Give me some advice like you're better than me. Ironically, friendship sometimes feels the same way to me. Huh, who knew?

```
```

I don't trust therapists. What kind of human profits from other people's misery? They're the lawyers of the mind, the psychos of the psyche.

```
```

A lot's on my mind a lot. My faith is made a mockery by the people who taught it to me. I grew up in a day where I had to learn to think outside the lines and redefine the world around me. Nothing should scare you like someone who speaks their mind.

My mind's lot is on a lot. A girl broke my heart, because believe it or not I didn't open up to her. Noticing a trend? She doesn't have a fucking clue mind you. Now I'm just bitter and that sucks too. There's this other girl who I've been thinking about recently, but I can't help but feel a little guilt, because well I've sorta been ignoring her. Ha, notice a trend? But I do think you're cute. Will I learn from my mistakes or are they what's going to stop me from liking you (because I kinda do).

Every week I feel wiser and taller. I didn't want to mature but was forced to. I'm a better person now, but I don't always know if I'm a happier one.

I try to not regret anything because the past made me, me. But I'm still learning to let go of it. I was raised on fairy tales and happy endings, but I wasn't ready for the story to never end. I'm a writer because that's when I get to control the narrative. Life is mine, but there's no autocorrect. It's like I said, music is my therapy.

```
```

My biggest fear isn't for you because it's what's true. When I need therapy, I want something new. I'm not trying to be blue, all I need is a clue. Ask about me, I'll say who?

I don't trust therapists. What kind of human profits from other people's misery? They're the lawyers of the mind, the psychos of the psyche.

Dear you, what do you say? Life is our therapy; will you be here with me? I don't let people in often, but I let people go less. This world ain't just our own. A friend for a friend, we're in this life together.

```
```

P.S. Hey all therapists, I'm sorry for what I said. I realize you're human too (probably), so please don't ignore my calls. Seriously, I left my jacket in your office. I apologize for insulting your entire institution, I mean it! Pinky promise! Fine then, be like that. *What a bunch of psychos...*

One Day I'll Know

Act III

The part where I was ready to find out.

A Caravan of One By Joshua Crocker

A man from Kentucky nearly lost his mind,
so he threw his suitcase in the back
and turned the radio on,
and before the crack of dawn
the next morning he was gone.
A man from Kentucky hit the road,
he was driving west when it started to snow,
he said to himself, "In life you'll never know,"
but y'know, that's just how this story goes.

He ducked into Tennessee, but it freaked him out.
He started to leave, that's when he saw a pretty SUV.
So, he made a stop to fill up his tank,
pretty SUV girl stepped out and gave him a wink,
he walked over and asked, "Where you from?"
She said, "Hun, I'm from Missouri son."
"Over there the people are nice, it's quite the home."
After he paid the gas, it was time to go.
Nothing happened in an SUV,
it was just a chance encounter,
he never stayed around long enough
for anything to flounder.

With nowhere to be, he made his way to a place,
"That's quite the home."
He spent his time in Missouri,
the whole time it brought him nothing but misery.
Just then it started to get cold
and just like his soul, it was gonna freeze,
so he knew it was time for him to leave.

A man from Kentucky hit the road
and y'know, that's just how this story goes:
A bottle of Appalachian bourbon shaking around,
driving through a town, an interurban braking sound.
He's making rest at an inn and truck stop,
finding a diner for dinner, dessert, and pop.
Route map, hacky sack, state song, shiny rocks.
He's living life as a caravan of one,
nothing else sounds quite as fun.

A bit further north was Iowa, despite his worries,
he kept singing along, la-la-la-la-la-la.
Corn was everywhere, met you from ear to ear,
what came next was a show,
grab your popcorn and let's go.
He landed in Des Moines and took a look in his
rearview mirror and told himself, "Ya foine."
His confidence yet to be shaken,
but the next part it was up for the takin'.
He made his way to a fan-say diner,
they served cornbread with their taters.
Quite the occasion.
He found a booth with a sassy waiter,
who asked what it for you:
"Steak meal or the chicken fingers?"
Was it even a question?
He enjoyed the food and apple pie al a mode,
but then he met his furry friend, and oh no.
Under the bar was a ratty fellow, he leaned in to say hi,
just then it attacked him.
A racoon bit his hands and he screamed,
Ahhhhhhhhhhhhhhhhhhhhhhhhhhhhhhhhhhhhhhh!
On the left it took the covenant and flippin' fingers.
On the right it took his pinky. Hell no.
That racoon was quite the kinky fellow.

Minnesota was the place for him to go,
a mint 'n soda made for an explosive combo.
After his little gas station treat
he needed to make a retreat.
This quaint college town was just down the road,
so he sped there a little too fast, uh-oh.
Mr. Copper flashed a light and pulled him over,
oh great, all he needed was this exposure.
Ticket or book it, urgency was still his matter,
he was a bit cranky with the officer,
got him sent to the precinct.
He only had one request,
the directions to the bathroom,
before he shat all over himself. Dude, sheesh.

This nobody from Kentucky didn't mean much,
so they gave him a junior defense attorney.
The kid from the college tried his best
but the ticket, it didn't get dismissed.
The kid got to talkin',
he didn't want to be here anymore,
his studies weren't for him, and he just felt at a loss.
Our main character knew how he felt.

So, after the fines were paid,
they met and got to thinkin',
maybe all they needed was a change of scenery,
the icy storms of the north were depression at the best.
So, that was it,
the kid from the college got in the passenger seat
and the two were off lookin' for something better.
Or at the least, some shinier weather.

A man from Kentucky hit the road
and y'know, that's just how this story goes:
A bottle of Appalachian bourbon shaking around,
driving through a town, an interurban braking sound.
He's making rest at an inn and truck stop,
finding a diner for dinner, dessert, and pop.
Route map, hacky sack, state song, shiny rocks.
He's living life as a caravan of two,
they're looking for something to call new.

They stopped and said their howdy's to Teddy
and Abe, Jefferson, and good ol' Washington.
During their stop they did the laundry.
They felt like the first president.
They were washing a ton.

Nebraska in a passing afternoon,
they saw a billboard filled with enticement,
the kid from the college wanted to make a stop
but the driver gave him a lasting scoff.
They started fighting,
yelling, and cussing obscenities.
One wanted to keep driving,
the other a hotel with amenities.
Deep into the night they kept the chaos goin'
before deciding to keep the car in silence.
...
...
It was dawn and the kid said,
"Hey, maybe drop me off here?"
A man from Kentucky looked him in the eye,
"You sure?"
"It's for the best," he responded.
They went their separate ways that day.

Before he entered Kansas the world was in color
but once he crossed that border
the whole place went to black and white duller.
Maybe he didn't realize what he was missing
till it was gone, so he made a U-turn and went
looking for what he lost.

Back in the Cornhusker State he had to pay the cost.
He found the kid from the college
and had two words to say: "I'm sorry."
The kid smiled; he forgave him that day.

Back on the road now, it was still rocky, the two were
mending, but in a few miles, they would be bending.
Tornado Alley tossed the worst at them,
they missed the warning and were driving
towards the twister, now mister,
if you find yourself in a blister, don't resist her.
The storm shook them, rain pouring down,
debris soaring around.
For a second they thought they were going to die,
this was it, the cruel end to a cruel life,
no time for goodbye.
Then they saw the light,
unsure if it was Heaven or lightning-lit skies.
They took a deep breath
and realized they had made it out,
the sun peaked out from behind the clouds' clout,
it was beautiful... but only for a moment.
They were about to find out this was no Heaven,
this was Oklahoma.

The wind came sweepin' down the plain in
Oooaak-la-homa!
The places there were as plain as a coma.
They made their way to the state's center,
there they found a pretty okay city,
the people there were drear nobodies
that anyone would pity.
Call it storm damage or travel wear,
but their car broke down,
all this traveling stress built up
and the two did the same.
They abandoned the car
and began walking around town,
the day started out optimistic,
but by the end it was all frowns.
The state of their journey would end in this stupid state,
this must be some cruel fate. A city to surely hate.
"This place sucks!" called out a man from Kentucky.
But maybe, just maybe, he was about to get lucky.

The boys saw a sign on a local store,
"Going out of business," surely this was forgiveness.
The two made their way inside,
behind the counter was this grandma from the city;
they asked her what was happening here,
she said times were tough, life can be rough.
Her store was closing, the last day before she was done.
Sympathetic they tried, but they were no better off,
she heard about their car troubles and scoffed,
"My friend's son is an auto mechanic.
I'll give him a call, peach."
The next morning he took a look,
got it fixed in the nick of time,
this awful place would take a toll on any bloke.
They paid the man what they had left,
leaving 'em broke.
Was this it? Even if they had a car,
they only had so much gas left in the tank.
What about food? Where would they sleep?
"Excuse me honeys, but I don't really have much
left for me here, do you think I could tag along?
See the country with y'all?"
It only took a moment to think,
this lady had been nothing but sweet.
She took what money she had left
and the three ditched that town in a heartbeat.

Finally, their time in Hell was over,
the people there were sad hicks
who couldn't put up a fight,
they left that place without finding
a hero or artist in sight.

A man from Kentucky hit the road
and y'know, that's just how this story goes:
A bottle of Appalachian bourbon shaking around,
driving through a town, an interurban braking sound.
He's making rest at an inn and truck stop,
finding a diner for dinner, dessert, and pop.
Route map, hacky sack, state song, shiny rocks.
He's living life as a caravan of three,
spendin' time on the road never felt so free.

They continued their journey west,
the plan was to see the coast and landmarks,
hopefully their efforts would be for the best.
They made their way through Texas.
Didn't stop for long, just for some gas,
some chicken 'n' waffles, and a night's rest at last.
Amarillo the perfect checkpoint,
the city creeped 'em out to their joints.
They got out there and
kept lookin' for the next sunset.

A new time zone, a new unknown.
The windows down and his left hand raised,
this country boy was a punk rocker for life.
Next they found Albuquerque a little quirky,
took a detour to the north,
would what they find there be worth the trip?

A girl from Santa Fe was living life on her own,
she was finding out who she was in this town.
Her dream of journalism
was turning into a search for her own internalism.
Everywhere she hit a wall,
no longer was she willing to take the fall.

One night she hit up a local bar,
a classy joint with a decent drink for a decent price.
A quiet night, she ordered a two shot
of cinnamon whiskey. For a Tuesday evening,
only a few other folks were getting frisky.
A girl from Santa Fe was thinking,
she was tired of the bureaucracy,
she wanted the freedom to explore,
write her own story for once.
Extra, extra, a new galore!

Just then, she noticed a few
out of towners sharing a booth,
they were getting a little rowdy, laughin'
and sharin' what's what.
She went over to say a little hello,
they welcomed her kindly,
asked her where she's from,
she replied, "I'm a girl from Santa Fe."
They smiled back at her.
"Well I'm a man from Kentucky."
The four got to chattin', sharing their life's story.
Just like her, they had seen their college dreams
fall away, a family they loved move across
the country to new towns, and just like her,
they had nearly lost their minds.
They told her she should hit the road, find a new hope.
She wasn't convinced, told them nope.
"I can make this work," she said.
So, they said good night and went away.

A girl from Santa Fe got back to her life
but this time it was different.
She couldn't find happiness in her work,
her whole career she had been looking to smirk
but never found it,
wasted her years not finding any luck.
She thought about what a few strangers told her,
so she grabbed her keys and hit the road.
She was driving west when the sun began to glow.
Maybe this was what she was destined to know.

Yeah... her trip didn't last long,
got a flat tire near the Canyon,
found a diner for dinner, in the town of Flagstaff.
While she was waiting for her food
she heard a familiar laugh,
she looked around and couldn't believe it,
it was those folks, the ones from before.
She went over and greeted them once more,
they invited her over to eat with them.

The four were talking like they were the best of friends.
She was across from a man
for whom she traded a glance with.
This man, once broken down by the weight of life,
he had found a new spark in him.
A new worth about him.
Every joke he told made her laugh for a mile
and when he heard her giggle,
he couldn't help but smile.
Once dinner was over, they were about to leave
when she suggested they stay for dessert,
reality is she wanted to continue the night with them.
So, they all ate their lemonade pie together,
something sweet.
After there were only crumbs left, they again began
to leave, when the man paused and turned back at
her, told her they had room in the backseat.
She thought. All she had was a flat
on her already old auto.
She was in. This time she tagged along for the fun.

They went up to see something Grand,
up there in desert land was a Canyon.
Quite the sight for a few nomads on a starry night.
This grandma from the city
was talking to the kid from the college,
told him he could do whatever he put his mind to,
he was bright young chap for whom she did care.
He was touched by her love and kindness,
so he asked about her life,
and boy, did she have stories to share.

Across the way the other two were giving
themselves a tour of the park,
they laughed and shared what life was to them.
Something had been missing for so long,
but tonight it felt right.
They talked about what they would find next, maybe
they would find home on the beaches of the coast,
but when they looked at the wonder in front of them,
maybe they knew they had already found it.
They almost missed, but before the night went,
they shared a kiss.

A man from Kentucky hit the road
and y'know, that's just how this story goes:
A bottle of Appalachian bourbon shaking around,
driving through a town, an interurban braking sound.
He's making rest at an inn and truck stop,
finding a diner for dinner, dessert, and pop.
Route map, hacky sack, state song, shiny rocks.
He's living life as a caravan of four,
now coming to the end of the tour.

Las Vegas for a quick night, played a few games,
won a few fights, grabbed a drink, and sang along.
Kept heading west to the City of Angels.
Missed a turn and wound up
surrounded by Joshua trees.
But y'know, they kept trucking on toward new seas.

Los Angeles was quite the place for sore eyes,
wonders around every corner,
they felt like a bunch of foreigners.
They spent a few days taking it all in,
tried the best restaurants,
visited a few beaches and even Disneyland,
then topped it with a movie
and a show from an A-list band.

This was it, their new home.
They all went looking for a job,
so together they could afford a one-bedroom place.
No luck for a single one of them to embrace.
After a week or so the novelty wore off,
they began to feel beat down and lost
almost exactly like they all did before.
They were nearly roped in by the bright lights
but they knew that they had to keep going.
LA was no home; it was time to keep growing.

It was late and they had just left the land of stars
but right now all they could see were the evening stars.
The two in the backseat were fast asleep
but a man and a girl in the front seat kept talking.
I'll leave the details of their
conversation for you to estimate,
what they said was genuine, sweet, and intimate.
Under the night sky and beam of car headlights
they said, "I love you," for the first time.

San Francisco and the bay, a wonderful delay.
They saw gold in the shade of red
and piers with their shares of bread.
By the time they left they grew worried,
Cascadia could be their last cascade.
They didn't have much room left to roam.

Would Oregon be their home,
or be gone would their hopes be?
Nope, they kept driving.
The days were getting rainy and wet, storm clouds
took the sun from them on the road you bet.

Washington at last. The great Pacific Northwest,
apples and coffee made for a neat breakfast.
They found a little town and began walking around.
A few nice parks, food was alright I guess.
The homes had a front door and a roof too, just in case.
Suburban roads said you could only travel 35 M-P-H.
They saw a quaint little place with a "For Sale" sign.
They grabbed lunch amongst the smell of pine,
while eating they discussed it, what do you say?
Maybe we've finally found it, our new home.

This town was no different than Kentucky,
college, the city, or even Santa Fe.
But they all of sudden seemed keen to settle down.
Had their destiny finally manifested in this town?
They had been living life on their own
looking for something new,
and finally they knew they had found it.
Here they were, a family.

A man from Kentucky hit the road,
he was driving west when it started to snow,
he said to himself, "In life you'll never know,"
but y'know, that's just how this story goes.
He met the kid from the college on his trip,
the two found a friend in each other, sharing quips.
In tornado alley they met this grandma from the city,
she had a way of making every single soul feel pretty.
A girl from Santa Fe was searching for life,
when she met a man running from strife.
The two got to talking
and before long were trading glances.
They fell in love one night on the road,
no longer were they lost and on their own.
It wasn't long before they all
decided to make Washington their home.

A man from Kentucky hit the road,
he had seen the highs of California
and the lows of Oklahoma,
but in the end wound up in a place not much different.
Yet he smiled, he never needed a new home,
he was only looking for a family of his own.
His girl and him were in love and there to stay,
they had a beauty named Sofia on the way.
He's living life as a caravan of five,
he had never felt so alive.

The Haunted Mansion By Joshua Crocker

Dear Lizzie, you're happy now
but you call me Mr. Misery.
I don't think so honey,
we're all happy haunts here.
You have 999 voices in your head,
where's the room for me?

I'll be your host.
Don't hang your head,
stand with pride and look alive.
No one is like you,
no one is as great as you.
We're here to survive,
we're here to thrive.
There's no turning back now.

Dear Lizzie, I tell you stories of a future,
a time when you're queen of your life,
I only remind you of the past to motivate,
all your darkest yearnings, I feel it too.
You shake your head,
tell me to shut up. I get it.
But do you?

Let me remind you,
you may be in control on the outside,
but up here, there are no windows and no doors.
All these voices echoing,
telling you each way to turn,
but you know deep down
that there's always my way out.
It's what you want, you know it.

Let this ambition grow in you,
happy haunts materialize and begin to vocalize,
instead your fears and anxiety have potentized,
and you're just the gullible fool who let them in.
I'm your friend, the one you can trust,
I just want what's best for you,
right now you're living for what?
I find it delightfully unlivable,
that's why I'll give you the vision of what's inexplicable.

Dear Lizzie, mortals pay a token fee,
but with me you may rest in peace, the haunting's free.
I'm the one who will never leave.
When your ghouls let you down,
I'll find you something never-ending.
Friends will abandon you when you fail,
so hurry back, you would like my company.

All these sounds around you,
start to shriek and harmonize,
hope, love, and happiness are lies.
You have 999 voices in your head,
where's the room for me?

When hinges creek in door chambers,
it's they who clammer.
Strange and frightening sounds echo through the halls,
that's their lying call.
Whenever candle lights flicker
where the air is deathly still,
it's the sign of the trickster's
fleeting care of deathly shrill.
That's the time when ghosts are present
practicing their terror with ghoulish delight.

Your cadaverous pallor betrays
an aura of foreboding,
almost as though you sense a
disquieting metamorphosis.
Those grim grinning ghosts may seem inviting
but heed this warning: The real chills come later.
What they tell you is a lie, a reassurance of failure
aided by sorrow and self-forgiveness.
I'll lead you on a quest of self-gratification
where there's no one who will
hold a candle to your majesty.

You think these walls are stretching?
You're running out of breath.
I think it's simply cozy.
What's life without a little death?

Now don't close your eyes and don't try to hide,
just stay by my side.
You say my voice can be terrifying?
Are you terrified of who you can be?
Are you terrified of the great things you see?
I'm just trying to let you be the best you,
isn't that what you said you're after?
Don't pretend my voice doesn't intrigue you,
I know it does.

Dear Lizzie, till death do us part.
In sickness and in this wealth.
For as long as we live,
and for better or your worse,
I do. And I did.

Last call, so you better stop running.
This is it, the greatness haunting you is ahead.
You have 999 voices in your head,
where's the room for me?

You foolish mortals can't see the greatness!
It's right in front of you, it makes me sick.
No more telling me to shut up, you prick!
I'm taking control tonight.
Mr. Misery, the ringing voice in your head,
call me Desire dear.

Paragon I By Joshua Crocker

He was a kid from Suburbia,
living the life of a Middle American hero,
and before long his very name would be proverbial.

Deep in the dark alleys of injustice,
stood a hero none like any other.
Metaphorically speaking he was a
shining light in the dark,
allegorically speaking he wore all
black and was filled with snark.
He would carry a heavy legacy with him thereon,
a superhero, they called him Paragon.

His origin story is formulaic of the skeptic,
he drank from a bottle of formula's synthetic.
It was on a high school field trip with friends.
PES-17 from a lab, PTSD from a stab,
gave Auhsoj Rekcorc the power
to hide from his problems.
Invisibility hindered to him hostility,
gave him the responsibility to up still his ability.

He designed the first suit he wore,
black from head to toe
with sleeves of bright green to strike woe.
He was given the power to hide,
he earned the power to fight,
trained in Karate and Tae Kwon Do,
learned to defend in Krav Maga and Judo.
Wore katana blades and kept his belt close to his hip
filled with gadgets to take out the dangerest of foes.

Deep in the dark alleys of injustice,
stood a hero none like any other.
Stopped a few robbers and muggers
here and there,
started to become a local lore legend,
bad guys beware!
He would carry a heavy legacy with him thereon,
a superhero, they called him Paragon.

Back to a lab nearby, in a place called Appleby
was a scientist with a misplaced sense of pride.
Dr. Nickels, was he unhinged or unforgiven?
Regardless, he seemed livid.
An underling's project had gotten out,
created a hero he had no control over.

So, he went back to drawing board,
recreated the power he wanted for him,
the power of power was what he was after.
His first victims were helpless,
they came to him for help.
He created a demon and a brute,
they were unforgivable he said.
These lost souls were given a second chance,
for that they would get a shot to enhance.
His desire for power was a success;
his mind the best, his heart a facade,
more than ever he felt like a god.

Paragon's legend grew and grew,
all he needed was an opposite.
Only where the dark consumes,
can a light thrive, and a hero die.
Just then, he heard the alert!
Two men taking part in the commencement of a crime,
across town they were stealing sciency supplies.
Paragon rushed to the scene,
there they were, the two from before.

One got in and out in a flash,
a true Speed Demon.
The other took out the guards with a wink,
a Powerhouse you see.
Fast feet and muscles chiseled,
villainous actions these two held,
only a hero could thwart them.
So that who does good is compelled.

A fight like none other happened that night,
Pow's and Ka-blam's,
Paragon snuck in from behind,
a side kick from the side,
a roundhouse to the face of Powerhouse,
the showdown had begun.
Speed Demon zoomed around dodging it all,
and Paragon knew if the other landed a hit,
well, he'd be done.
But the invisible sneak had a plan,
he retreated to the shadows,
leaving the two flunkies to their follies.
And then Bam! He threw the runner into a wall
and a perfectly landed uppercut to the jaw of Mr. Tall.
The lackeys barely escaped with a lack of success.
When they got back the boss man was not impressed.

Deep in the dark alleys of injustice,
stood a hero none like any other.
Defeated the supervillains of society
without a doubt,
from here on out, when danger is present
he'll stand stout.
He would carry a heavy legacy with him thereon,
a superhero, they called him Paragon.

Auhsoj returned to his home.
The kid had lost a lot before,
said goodbye to his doggy best friend,
never met his beautiful baby sister,
and his parents hadn't made it from the fire.
But now he had a purpose for the pain,
maybe this was always the plan.
No longer would the people of Appleby hurt,
for their superhero was watching out for them.

Auntie Grace and Uncle David had taken him in,
it was the place he called home.
They were scientists by profession,
but his family at heart.
Cousin Noah was like a little brother to Auhsoj,
the two threw a football around in the frontyard.

This is what he fought for.
A light in the darkness,
a paragon of love for another,
a hero like none other.

This wasn't his last issue,
rather a shiny #1 of what was to come.
Mint-sleeved, the dawn and origin story of Paragon.
In a world filled with science, magic,
and all that's cosmic,
tune in to the action and adventure
of a superhero with wit like the comics.

Deep in the dark alleys of injustice,
stood a hero none like any other.
He was just a kid,
a freshman in high school,
nothing special about him,
but that mask was his secret jewel.
He would carry a heavy legacy with him thereon,
a superhero, they called him Paragon.

540 By Joshua Crocker

You're driving down life's highway
drunk behind the wheel,
my best friend for-whatever is a moronic idiot.
The kid I once knew took a five-forty turn,
now I'm going to watch as your world burns.
You got what you wanted,
are you happy now?

Woah-oh-err-ahh-yeah! Take it back!

You're exactly who your parents said you'd be.
Y'know, I stood up for you when no one else did,
look where that got me.
It turns out everyone was right about you,
you're livin' the cliché stereotype,
life turned upside-down, deal with the hype!
You're a selfish motherfucker,
look where that got you.

If you call my best friend a bitch one more time,
I'll toss you out of my car and slap you fine.
She's two times the person you'll ever be.
Welcome to life. You feeling alive?

Oh-oh-no-oh-ho! Yo!
Feeling dizzy!
You made a five-forty!
This is it, oh!
You made a five-forty!
Deal with it for me,
oh-oh-no-oh-ho!

You're driving down life's highway
drunk behind the wheel,
my best friend for-whatever is a moronic idiot.
The kid I once knew took a five-forty turn,
now I'm going to watch as your world burns.
You got what you wanted,
are you happy now?

Woah-oh-err-ahh-yeah! Take it back!

We were once two sunbaked kids in the backseat,
girly name-calling and laughing,
har-dee-har-ha and look now.
That's the person you once were,
I trusted you like a brother,
why now it's whatever,
we had something special I guess.
You were a little selfish then and a lotta selfish now.
I've got one more name for you bitch.

Don't tell me how to treat who I love,
I'll take advice from you when pigs die,
you treat people like objects to scoff at
and I'm looking for someone who cares.
So for now, goodbye.

Oh-oh-no-oh-ho! Yo!
Feeling dizzy!
You made a five-forty!
This is it, oh!
You made a five-forty!
Deal with it for me,
oh-oh-no-oh-ho!

You're driving down life's highway
drunk behind the wheel,
my best friend for-whatever is a moronic idiot.
The kid I once knew took a five-forty turn,
now I'm going to watch as your world burns.
You got what you wanted,
are you happy now?

Woah-oh-err-ahh-yeah! Take it back!

I'm sure you've heard it all before,
I hardly recognize you anymore.
And I'm not about to mince by words,
we're in this game of who's who
and I'm still playing not to lose,
now I ask you this: How about you?

I think my friend is gone,
I lost him some time ago.
Do you recognize yourself in the mirror?
Because if this is you,
then I'm sorry for what comes next,
because this very well may be it.

Oh-oh-no-oh-ho! Yo!
Feeling dizzy!
You made a five-forty!
This is it, oh!
You made a five-forty!
Deal with it for me,
oh-oh-no-oh-ho!

You're driving down life's highway
drunk behind the wheel,
my best friend for-whatever is a moronic idiot.
Fuck you!
The kid I once knew took a five-forty turn,
now I'm going to watch as your world burns.
You got what you wanted.
Are you happy now?
Are you happy now?
Are you happy now?
You've taken a five-forty turn,
time to watch it all burn.

Oh!

Oh!

Oh!

Oh!

Oh!

Oh!

Oh!

No!

Hey dude, I hope you've gotten help.
You have your whole life ahead of you,
don't throw it away.
I'll always love you man,
and you know how to find me.
You don't need another one-eighty,
just a degree at a time.

My Thoughts Written Down By Joshua Crocker

Hey, do you have a minute? I had something kinda crazy I wanted to tell you.

I'm gonna be honest, being honest about how I feel isn't easy. Weak in the knees, butterflies in my stomach, kinda queasy. Every time I see you, I want to tell you how much I like you.

These are my thoughts written down, so when I talk to you, I don't forget what I wanted to say.

I sometimes imagine taking you on our first date. I've never really cared what we're doing, the only part that matters is you next to me. We could grab a bite to eat, visit a library, or just sit around watching TV. I'd say something dumb, and you could just laugh at me. Ha, I'm sitting here laughing at myself.

These are my thoughts written down, as a reminder to not let you go this time, without me saying this to you.

Hey, I think you're cute, just to let you know. It's a takedown, why do I always feel like I let myself down? Do you notice how I always look your way? Or how at the end of the night before I leave, I'm too afraid to stop and say how amazing I find you?

These are my thoughts written down because you're the one on my mind in time. Why then am I scared to ask you out?

Maybe sometimes I feel stupid for having feelings. I have no reason why I do, just my anxiety telling me what's not true. But when I talk with you, I just can't stop thinking about how great tonight is. That's why I'm thinking here, I want to be your friend, because being around you never feels wrong.

These are my thoughts written down, the thoughts that keep me thinking about you. I know what I want to tell you, and yet for some reason I'm still trying to find the words to say.

I'm sorry that I'm keeping my thoughts to myself. You deserve me being honest with you. I'm sorry that I don't have it figured out. The tendencies in me tell me to be an anxious, perfectionist, hopeless romantic. I'm so worried about little things that don't matter and making sure what I write down is the perfect story, when I don't care about any of that. I just want to put my arm around you and talk about whatever, it really doesn't matter if you're smiling up at me.

These are my thoughts written down, when I see you next, I'll tell them to you.

I'm sorta figuring out this new side of me. I'm no longer a kid who can't tell the difference between things. My thoughts are complicated and all over the place, but I know I want you there. This is the way I feel, so I'm ready to not be scared of thoughts that are real to me.

These are my thoughts written down because writing is the most honest part of me. I think you're pretty and I like you too. Just so you know.

Do you ever think about me? Maybe I'm worried I don't mean as much to you as you do to me. If you don't, it'll be okay. Oh whom I kidding, I shouldn't be writing sappy lyrics like this. My writing is better than this. Or is it?

Hey, do you have a minute? I have these thoughts to say out loud. It may sound crazy, but that's how I feel about you.

I Hate School By Joshua Crocker

What's the factorial of five?
What were the restoration colonies?
Questions on a test, words on a paper.
Ugh, I don't care.
The boiling point of water in Kelvin,
mnemonic devices to remember planets,
nothing about this even matters!

Hey!
Mom and dad are proud!
I got another A on some test,
I didn't really study,
why be bothered
when I can pass in record time!
Essays riddled with red marks
but in my poems, I can mispeel all I want!
Probably have an undiagnosed focus disorder,
doodled a map in my brain
and skimmed the page because reading's hard,
I rather listen to music and write!
History and language arts are a waste
when I could be doing karate, hi-ya!

Spent days at the library from K-8th grade,
I was a top student in high school,
and now I'm working on a college degree,
but oh, ya know,
I still hate school.
Oh, ya know, I hate school.
Oh, ya know, I hate school.
This assignment drools,
doodling sports scores rules,
becuz, oh, ya know, I hate school!

Give me 120 reasons why I should be here,
I could be in New York or Pennsylvania,
seeing the coast in New Jersey and Carolina.
My head's spinning 373.1 degrees around,
just thirteen and a tenth extra,
a little bit more for good measure.
My vast encyclopedic mastery
just seems useless nerd. (Perhaps.)

Five paragraphs exact for an essay,
the subject matter on post-colonial tensions;
it's a bit hard to give my jovial attention,
when my writing is amazing, so says I,
I'm creative and expressive
and school likes to put a lid on all of that.
I mean, I still simply do not care,
so I'll watch Netflix as I study.
But yet, guess what my grades are?
A for awesome, astounding, and amazing.
Lol.

I could have got into any college in the country
but I didn't send in a single application.
They may say I'm not applying myself,
I do have a tendency of procrastination,
but is my future really in a lit and comp lecture?
Teaching people to kick and using my imagination
is what I'm after.

Hey!
Mom and dad are proud!
I got another A on some test,
I didn't really study,
why be bothered
when I can pass in record time!
Essays riddled with red marks
but in my poems, I can mispeel all I want!
Probably have an undiagnosed focus disorder,
doodled a map in my brain
and skimmed the page because reading's hard,
I rather listen to music and write!
History and language arts are a waste
when I could be doing karate, hi-ya!
Spent days at the library from K-8th grade,
I was a top student in high school,
and now I'm working on a college degree,
but oh, ya know,
I still hate school.
Oh, ya know, I hate school.
Oh, ya know, I hate school.
This assignment drools,
doodling sports scores rules,
becuz, oh, ya know, I hate school!

I spend as much time actually studying
as the characters on Community.
Coincidentally the same show I watched
as I aced my last test.
I go outside to throw a football around,
I've got an excel sheet with all the stats,
over 200 player names, box scores, and standings
of my make-believe football league from 2217.

I'm writing songs instead,
thinking one day I'll know why I'm here.
When I really care about something,
that's when I give it my all,
and this just simply ain't that.
The education of life isn't in a classroom,
a pile of homework, or a meeting on Zoom.
But here I am, and I know I'll give it my best.
Because it feels like my best is all I got.

Others can be jealous of me,
I would be too. ~~I'm that cool, really.~~
I can absently go through the motions
and still succeed. ~~I guess I'm just a genius.~~
My mind never stops running,
I have trouble keeping up to be honest,
call it ADHD, I don't like sitting still,
but whatever I say, I like it this way.

Hey!
Mom and dad are proud!
I got another A on some test,
I didn't really study,
why be bothered
when I can pass in record time!
Essays riddled with red marks
but in my poems, I can mispeel all I want!
Probably have an undiagnosed focus disorder,
doodled a map in my brain
and skimmed the page because reading's hard,
I rather listen to music and write!
History and language arts are a waste
when I could be doing karate, hi-ya!
Spent days at the library from K-8th grade,
I was a top student in high school,
and now I'm working on a college degree,
but oh, ya know,
I still hate school.
Oh, ya know, I hate school.
Oh, ya know, I hate school.
This assignment drools,
doodling sports scores rules,
becuz, oh, ya know, I hate school!

Sitting on a pew at church
I imagine a society on the high rise,
little people on adventures,
I can't keep up with the preacher,
listening to him speak for this long is so boring.
Sunday morning class meant nothing
until a teacher let me say something.

Tests ain't hard if you game the system,
educated guessing is the best thing I learned.
Math when I hold the key is a cool hobby.
X times Y equals Z, and my favorite projects
are the ones where I got to design something.

Okay! Enough, let's study.
Hmm-hmm-hmm.
I wonder what's for lunch? No, focus...
Ooh! I just thought of a good line for a song,
I'll just write it down real quick.
Yawn! Woah, I've been working for like 20 minutes.
Time for break, I should have a marble race,
maybe design a promo card for my new game.

Hey!
To all the kids out there
who are a lot like me,
maybe try to do a little studying.
You gotta give this your best shot
because no matter what you're good at,
you've got something about you to be proud about.
School may or may not be a waste,
I wouldn't really know,
but get better at what you got,
become the greatest writer or sports player,
maybe a hit singer or martial arts instructor,
find something worth all of your amazing thoughts.

But oh, ya know,
I still hate school.
Oh, ya know, I hate school.
Oh, ya know, I hate school.
This assignment drools,
doodling sports scores rules,
becuz, oh, ya know, I hate school!

The Separation of Church and State By J. Crocker

Eeee-ahhh! Ahhhh-arghh-ahhh! Uuahhahh!
Cock it.

Oh, my dear,
here's my fear:
one nation under God,
run by ignorant frauds
voted in by the people of love.
Oh. How. Fun.
You better grab a gun.

Oh-oh-oh!
It's the separation of church and state,
the expiration of control and hate.
Lies and fear are weapons here.
Oh-oh-oh!
It's our respiration of a heartbeat,
the desperation in my song beat.
Love is the bullet in your mirror.
Bssh-t-t-t-chk!

Fair warning,
what I'm about to say may be controversial
but I don't fucking care.
And my wordage isn't by bondage,
so don't get up and antsy
just because you can't handle a little swearing.
This is a declaration
of where we went wrong,
so listen to this song
and maybe stop fainting at a little blood.
After all, you let it fall.

Don't talk to me about honoring my family name
when you call yourself a Christian,
where's the honor for your father? Huh man?
What a sham shame.

The men and women of faith,
you're the self-titled heroes of our culture,
your conviction is stronger than life's tides
in a world where all you see is heathenistic sin.
Set apart from the rest?
Give me a fucking break,
you don't even know what you believe in!

You quote the Bible like the constitution:
without knowing a damn thing
about what you're reading.

Mental health?
Haharhaha, we all knows that's not real.
Just be happy, that's the deal.
I mean sure it'd be easier if things weren't so cynical,
but when the air sucks and bandages are for the rich
your head starts to feel clinical.
So, if you want to play this game, fine.
Let's do it. Let's get political.

Oh-oh-oh!
It's the separation of church and state,
the expiration of control and hate.
Lies and fear are weapons here.
Oh-oh-oh!
It's our respiration of a heartbeat,
the desperation in my song beat.
Love is the bullet in your mirror.
Bssh-t-t-t-chk!

Your teens are crying, nearly dying,
tears covering our bedsheets,
blood under our shirtsleeves.
You wanna know somethin' funny?
When you tell someone they're unloved,
they feel like no one loves them.

If you don't like something it's a "lifestyle,"
because apparently choosing to be gay
is a valid excuse to not serve someone a cake
or a piece of paper that comes with tax cuts.
Stop using religion to be a dick.
Oh, and it's not a choice jerks.
Lifting our skirts doesn't make you a pervert
because you're just "protecting the kids."
Haha, we all know that's not true.

Woah! There's two kinds of people:
you, the heroic Christian,
and the drug-abusin', sex-havin', atheistic,
gamblin', prideful, sinful, rockstar bastards.
No in between?
A little black and white if you ask me,
maybe get outside every once and a while,
have an open mind and find someone new.
Even with my social anxiety,
I'd say meeting people is cool.

I'm sorry to say the sexually repressed
are the ones gatekeeping what to wear.
You can try to teach modesty
or you can learn to live with respect.
It goes both ways.

They won't teach it in schools
becuz abstinence is their way to go.
They won't teach it at home
becuz it's better to stay pure.
They're all immature you say,
well, you never taught them to mature,
instead you just kick out your daughter
when she dares to get pregnant.

Oh-oh-oh!
It's the separation of church and state,
the expiration of control and hate.
Lies and fear are weapons here.
Oh-oh-oh!
It's our respiration of a heartbeat,
the desperation in my song beat.
Love is the bullet in your mirror.
Bssh-t-t-t-chk!

You put the Ten Commandments
outside of the court room,
yet you idolize your made-up hero,
I'm not sure about you,
but I did a little fact-checking,
and you might want to check out Exodus 20,
that's a two then a zero.
You think it's funny you elected a hypocrite?
Now is it supposed to be funny to see your hissy-fit?

You wanna keep politics out of the church?
Then how about you keep the church out of politics?
Seems fair, a hardy dare.

You've blurred the line between
evangelism and conservatism,
a capitalist empire is your lovely idea,
say commercialism, an economic ideal
based off men's desire for money,
excuse me honey, but that seems quite contrary,
for the love of money is the root of evil,
I mean it says so in your Bible, check 1 Timothy.
Did you know the early Christian folk shared,
I remember back in pre-k learning that feat,
but hey, you've rebranded it as the dastardly socialism.
You do realize just because faith is a thing,
doesn't require you to abandon logicism.

What about us: the everyday family?
You're against abortion
and all for family supportion,
but only when dad's at work
and mom's in the kitchen will it work.
The rest of us are struggling
in our broken homes with single parents
or our two moms we can't talk about.
You only care about kids before they're born
or when they're sitting in your class indoctrination.
You take from the poor to give to the rich
for your fixed system of class incongruity.
Instead of fixing the problem
you're taking away the solution.
For James 1:26-2:13,
bridle the tongue, religion undefiled:
visit the orphans and widows,
partiality our sin, for a gold ring ain't better,
don't disregard the poor,
after all the rich disregard you,
mercy triumphs over judgement too.

Oh-oh-oh!
It's the separation of church and state,
the expiration of control and hate.
Lies and fear are weapons here.
Oh-oh-oh!
It's our respiration of a heartbeat,
the desperation in my song beat.
Love is the bullet in your mirror.
Bssh-t-t-t-chk!

Oh. Fuck. Gasp!
Won't somebody think of the children?!
Because you're feeding them to the wolves!
You've found a second assmendin' dogma to worship.
This one makes me mad.
How's it feel to have tried nothing
and things are still bad?
Get your priorities straight
you inconceivable selfish bastards!

Ever read Luke 9:23 or Matt 16:24?
You've put down your cross for a firearm,
turns out ignoring pain is surprisingly easy
when you're the one dealing harm.
You misquote a book
to back a misrepresented history,
what that flags stands for is nothing of note,
so stop flying it above your steeple,
and start protecting and caring for your people.
This is greater than one nation,
it's not about one generation,
start in Acts 10:34 for the correlation.
That's what your faith is about. Isn't it?

Ba-ba-bang!
Hear that now!
It's the gunshot of love and peace!
Hide! This is our exasperation of control and hate!
It's the damnation of church and state!
Ooohhhhhhhaaahhhhhhh! Bssh-t-t-t-chk!

We're coming to the end of the song,
so you can stop covering your kids' ears now.
I'm a Christian and my fear is this:
I lost you because maybe what I said was wrong.
I'm only a kid trying to be a light when it feels dark.
I want to quote my life with John 15:13,
"Greater love has no one than this:
to lay down one's life for one's friends."
And I'll be doing that till the end.

I Can't Get You Off My Mind By Joshua Crocker

Hey, I like you. I really do.
I wasn't sure at first, but now I know it's true.
I've always thought you were kinda cute
and y'know, lately I can't take my eyes off you.
You're the song stuck in my head
when I'm walking at night listening to sappy music.
Your voice echoes through my thoughts
and y'know, I can't get you off my mind.

I'm chewing strawberry lemonade gum,
I wrote your name on the inside of the wrapper
surrounded by little hearts and a tree.
You have a pretty name. And I like drawing trees.

Our inside jokes and stories are my favorite,
you never fail to be anything less than photogenic,
maybe that's why a picture of you is always in my head,
maybe that's why I wish you were my screensaver too.

There was this one evening I said goodbye,
after you left, I muttered to myself,
"Damn, she's so awesome."
After I talk with you, I just stop and smile.

Hey, I like you. I really do.
I wasn't sure at first, but now I know it's true.
I've always thought you were kinda cute
and y'know, lately I can't take my eyes off you.
You're the song stuck in my head
when I'm walking at night listening to sappy music.
Your voice echoes through my thoughts
and y'know, I can't get you off my mind.

Sometimes I'm a bit of a confident, snarky loner,
but around you I'm a nervous, giggling mess.
Ha, you say the dumbest stuff and I'll still laugh,
you're a dork and that's why talking to you is the best.

I wanna take a stroll in a park
holding your hand close to mine,
I'll read this song I wrote for you,
let you know how much your smiles shines.

Hey, I'm sorry if I seem a little extra,
I get anxious when talking to you,
sometimes I say the weirdest stuff,
but when you leave it's never enough.

Hey, I like you. I really do.
I wasn't sure at first, but now I know it's true.
I've always thought you were kinda cute
and y'know, lately I can't take my eyes off you.
You're the song stuck in my head
when I'm walking at night listening to sappy music.
Your voice echoes through my thoughts
and y'know, I can't get you off my mind.

You keep me thinking,
of all my thoughts, the one's with you are the best.
I don't think of memories and hope as the enemy
if it means your there just as well.

This may sound a little crazy I say,
but there's something about you
that makes me happy to see you.
You should see how I smile when you text me.

I'm trying to finish this song,
this is the time I'll tell you about how I feel,
you and I together is what I keep dreaming,
so under the light of the night, here we are.

Hey, I like you. I really do.
I wasn't sure at first, but now I know it's true.
I've always thought you were kinda cute
and y'know, lately I can't take my eyes off you.
You're the song stuck in my head
when I'm walking at night listening to sappy music.
Your voice echoes through my thoughts
and y'know, I can't get you off my mind.

I can't get you off my mind,
the way you laugh and smile,
the way my hearts melts when you're nearby,
the way I feel about you.

You're the song stuck in my head,
the one with my favorite rhythm
that I hum along too all the time,
with these poorly written lyrics of mine
about how I can't get you off my mind.

Oh, oh, la-la-la.

I can't get you off my mind,
the way you laugh and smile,
the way my hearts melts when you're nearby,
the way I feel about you.

Oh, oh, la-la-la. This is the song I'm singing.

Hey, I like you. I really do. ♡

This song is stupid. Shut up. No you shut up. Can't you get back to writing about the flawed impact of a theocratic state? Can't get you back to not being dumb. Nice comeback. Thanks. That was sarcasm. Well, I like to think this was a very sweet song. Maybe if you think cough syrup is sweet. Haha, you're sooo funny. Do you even know who this song is about? Umm… no, but that's aside the point. So, you wrote a song that's not even true? Well, it wouldn't be my first time.

Parties By Joshua Crocker

There's a party this Saturday
but I rather just stay home.
But then I'll be sad and alone,
so I'll go instead and hate it anyway.
I feel lonelier around people I don't like
and the people I like never come,
I hate them for that, it's dumb.
So, I'll make small talk until something big strikes.

Pop!
Each balloon drops.
Pop! Pop! Pop!

I mumble and stumble,
laugh it off,
keep walking,
keep talking,
you never know when they'll strike,
anxious, impatient,
keep it going,
never stopping,
never going anywhere,
except here.

I stick to the cookie and punch table,
the "they beat me to the punch" fable.
I rather just watch everyone else's story,
like a sitcom TV show or people-watching evening.
Outside of the spotlight leaves me no worry,
here's my story: an intentional absence of feeling.

Pop!
Each balloon drops.
Pop! Pop! Pop!

I'm a bit shaky,
probably from that coffee,
why are we laughing?
It's sorta funny,
I started talking,
first, I thought,
then I lost it,
but I own it,
phoned it,
I'm here,
they hear,
but where is there?

There's this trend I've noticed since middle school,
wherever I sit, is where everyone else isn't,
and I'm kinda okay with that. Mostly...
It sure is less scary than talking to people,
but I still feel left out when I hear all the chatter,
wondering if I were sitting with them,
maybe I could talk myself into fitting right in.

Pop!
Each balloon drops.
Pop! Pop! Pop!

New friends,
new memories,
someone I knew,
is now gone,
but they're right here too,
relative to the night,
nothing is right,
but in life, tonight,
is what I'll want,
so I thought,
but this is what I got.
Huh.

Truth is, I'm happy to be here.
Home is nice and cozy,
I have hideaways where everything is rosy,
but stepping outside my doors, won't leave tears.
This smile I have really is real,
I'm anxious, impatient, but laughing too,
I'm no longer afraid of something new.
I'm glad to see you, and that's how I really feel.

Pop!
Each balloon drops.
Pop! Pop! Pop!

Smile,
no more denial,
people lie too,
you're in your head,
be in this place.
Let's go to the party.
Let go and party.
All they want is to be liked by you
and that's what you want too.
Smile. And breath.
Pop. The last balloon drops.
See you soon, :)

I Knew Spring By Joshua Crocker

It's a new spring, and the world feels alright. Me and the birds will sing, and I'll dance in a park at night. I'm driving in the rain with my brand new eyes. The trees shout all that's green, my favorite color to see. I'm back to dreaming of watching the sunset, just that girl and me. I'd be a fool to put it all in words, dare you do the impossible to describe a feeling. A smile on my face and a beat in my heart because I knew spring.

Hey, baby brother I just gotta ask: What's it like to run around without a care? This beautiful spring morning let's take a day to forget the mourning. Let's take a day to hide away in the semi-pretty parks of our suburban dream. Flip it on its head and nothing's what it seems.

It's a new spring, thank you God for loving me every day. I see glory in the colors around me.

When my optimism keeps me afloat, it at the best lets me thrive. I stand by it; the world is a canvas, and my life is my greatest story. The pen, it's a gateway, so I'll keep the key close to my heart, right there next to my thoughts. Music is the locket around my arm, each song a capsule of emotion's blot.

It's a new spring, thank you God for loving me every day. I see glory in the colors around me.

Some days I feel like a hopeless romantic. I use poetry to ascribe some sense from the semantic. My words catch up to me; I can write, but I can't sing. It didn't stop me from writing a song to the girl with a pretty face, because I can't get her off my mind. I can hear your infectious laugh through a mask. I wonder if an aurora shines as bright as you. You're weird in the most familiar way, the same way I feel around you. I'll write my thoughts down, so I don't forget what to say.

It's a new spring, and the world feels alright. Me and the birds will sing, and I'll dance in a park at night. I'm driving in the rain with my brand new eyes. The trees shout all that's green, my favorite color to see. I'm back to dreaming of watching the sunset, just that girl and me. I'd be a fool to put it all in words, dare you do the impossible to describe a feeling. A smile on my face and a beat in my heart because I knew spring.

Skipping stones, it's my time to atone. I feel anxious at parties and scared when it's dark and lonely. I doodle a map of my own world in my brain; I'm not focusless, I just focus less. There are 999 voices in my head. I'll lay across the grass, cloud gazing, but if I get distracted than I'll know I'm still me. I'm afraid of the dark, because I'm afraid of dealing with my insecurities, falling in the depths of sin. I know I get anxious and impatient; I wonder do you like me? My therapist tells me to open up anyway. Thankfully, spring's leaves leave me calmer. I'm the psycho of the psyche when it comes to psyching myself out. Woo!

It's a new spring, thank you God for loving me every day. I see glory in the colors around me.

Just like these bees buzzing around here, you're going to have a hard time shutting me up. I know, I'll make a difference with what I say. When we know what the trouble is, I'll raise my hand to speak up. Oh, my dear, here's my fear: we don't act like it. It's time for the expiration of control of hate, this will be my fate.

It's a new spring, thank you God for loving me every day. I see glory in the colors around me.

Call me short, but I'm the one standing tall. I'm trying to be a paragon; a shining light in the dark. Friends have taken a five-forty, cuts and scars on their arms. I so hate consequences, they're my worst nemesis. Save me, I'm not dying, I'm thriving. I prefer the quiet parts of life, the call of birds and rings of cicadas. It's the nature and nurture of spring.

It's a new spring, and the world feels alright. Me and the birds will sing, and I'll dance in a park at night. I'm driving in the rain with my brand new eyes. The trees shout all that's green, my favorite color to see. I'm back to dreaming of watching the sunset, just that girl and me. I'd be a fool to put it all in words, dare you do the impossible to describe a feeling. A smile on my face and a beat in my heart because I knew spring.

I wrote a song about Christmas when I was afraid of growing up. If I grow up, will all the magic be lost? Once summer hits I'll be eighteen. My story's about to start and I'm afraid to stop reading the prologue. I say to myself, "In life you'll never know." But y'know, that's just how this story goes. Alright, alright, I've figured out who I want to be, and my teenage identity crisis is done. Yet may I ask how to live up to the expectation? Eh, forget it. As long I keep hoping for more days like today, rain showers and sunlight make for the perfect dream. Smile now, because we're all sitting around these spring trees. But I will say, these friggin' bugs better leave me the frick alone.

It's a new spring, thank you God for loving me every day. I see glory in the colors around me.

I held a door shut on a windy day and it got me thinking. You'll never hear it, but my first chorus isn't even true anymore. The trouble with my mind is it never stops. Your little white lies, I see you in my rearview mirror. Sometimes I just need you to leave me alone. I want to enjoy this wonderful evening, but I'm worried I'll let it escape by. Because right now I sit alone in my car unsure of where to go. But damn, feel that slight breeze. A paper capering pen with me. I'm sitting under the shady tree, listening to music and it's just me. I know this won't be my best poem, but I won't ever stop loving to write. And this isn't the perfect night, just another day in the perfect life for me.

It's a new spring, thank you God for loving me every day. I see glory in the colors around me.

It's a new spring, and the world feels alright. Me and the birds will sing, and I'll dance in a park at night. I'm driving in the rain with my brand new eyes. The trees shout all that's green, my favorite color to see. I'm back to dreaming of watching the sunset, just that girl and me. I'd be a fool to put it all in words, dare you do the impossible to describe a feeling. A smile on my face and a beat in my heart because I knew spring.

I wrote a song about Christmas when I was afraid of growing up. I held a door shut on a windy day and it got me thinking. You'll never hear it, but my first chorus isn't even true anymore. I feel anxious at parties and scared when it's dark and lonely. I wrote a song to my brother and the girl with a pretty face. I'm just a kid and I know one day I'll know. But I'll always know spring.

~ Poems and songs by
Joshua Crocker

Index

540	127
Act Like It	11
A Caravan of One	95
Damn Wind	27
Depths of Sin	77
Do You Like Me?	83
The Haunted Mansion	115
Hey, Baby Brother	7
I Can't Get You Off My Mind	155
I Can Write, But I Can't Sing	15
I Hate School	137
I Knew Spring	165
i'm still afraid of the dark	31
Leave Me Alone	79
Little White Lies	69

Middle America   65

My Last Christmas   41

My Thoughts Written Down   133

My Worst Nemesis   35

One Day I'll Know   49

Paragon I   121

Parties   161

The Pen, It's a Gateway   3

The Separation of Church and State   145

Shopping Mall   59

The Song You'll Never Hear   21

The Song You'll Never Hear (Reprise)   39

Sunspot Freckles   73

Therapist   87

The Trouble Is   55

Acknowledgements

So, I guess I'm supposed to write about people and things that influence me? C'mon, I just wrote 170 pages about all of that...

But really, thank you to everyone who helped be become the person I am today. *One Day I'll Know* was always about a kid taking the first step to becoming himself. No matter who you are, I hope you found words that spoke to you, whether it was a song or even just a paragraph.

Thank you mom and dad. Even in crazy times you never stopped loving me. You encouraged me to explore my own path and support me no matter who I am.

If there's anything as important to me as writing and creating, it's the relationships I have. To my friends, thank you for giving me a place other than my notebook where I can be me. Also, thanks for letting me write about y'all. I mean none of you gave me permission too, but what are you going to do about it? I also want to acknowledge anyone who's taught me something, whether it's how to kick higher in my katas, the difference between then and than, or how to read the Bible critically.

Joshua Crocker,
Author of One Day I'll Know

About the Author circa 2022

I am graphic designer focused on media, full-time martial arts instructor, and freelance writer. I have spent my whole life in suburban Oklahoma and do in fact, know what the interior of a tornado shelter looks like.

One Day I'll Know is the first full poem and song collection I have written, and my first published book. The collection includes 30 songs written from July 2021 to July 2022 (as well as a few of my early poems from years prior).

I enjoy spending my time teaching martial arts, writing at coffee shops or libraries, and making a few random projects with excel spreadsheets.

I hope everyone can find a way to express themself, through writing or whatever else they shine at. Don't be afraid to be passionate and stand up for what you believe in, always striving to be who you are.

I am currently working on several new writing projects. If you finished reading this book, then I'm excited for you get to read what I've got in store next.

> *"I can do all things through him who strengthens me."*
> - *Philippians 4:13*